LANGUAGE *from* HEAVEN

A Better Way to Get Your Prayers Answered

Dr. Goodluck Okotie-Eboh

WESTBOW
PRESS
A DIVISION OF THOMAS NELSON

WestBow Press books may be ordered through booksellers or by contacting:

WestBow Press
A Division of Thomas Nelson
1663 Liberty Drive
Bloomington, IN 47403
www.westbowpress.com
1-(866) 928-1240

ISBN: 978-1-4497-4969-9 (sc)
ISBN: 978-1-4497-4970-5 (e)
ISBN: 978-1-4497-4968-2 (hc)

Library of Congress Control Number: 2012919980

Printed in the United States of America

WestBow Press rev. date: 11/15/2012

Contents

Preface

One of the most frustrating things for a true seeker of the kingdom of God is to deal with conflicting positions on faith in key areas of the Christian life. There are conflicting positions in the doctrine of salvation: some believe you can never lose your salvation, while others believe that you can. Some believe that God still heals today, but others do not believe in healing. There are conflicting beliefs about whether or not there are apostles or prophets in the church today. Some believe that the Holy Spirit's gifts, as described in chapter 12 of 1 Corinthians, are still given to us today, but others wonder if that is true. The list goes on and on.

I struggled as a new Christian. I had to learn how to live and grow in my faith. Now my desire is to help, whenever possible, those who have a strong desire to grow in knowledge and wisdom in things pertaining to the kingdom of God. I am still learning and growing in the grace of our Lord. This book addresses the most powerful tool God gave Christians for living a victorious life: the power of language.

This book does not deal with the motivational gifts of the Holy Spirit as recorded in chapter 12 of Romans. These gifts differ from person to person according to the grace of God in the believer's life. A believer's gift is a clear sign of what the primary motivator for Christian service in the life of the believer is. It is what the believer majors in as a Christian—prophesying, serving, teaching, exhortation, giving, leading, or being merciful. Nor does this book address the gifts mentioned in Ephesians 4:11. These are the five-fold ministry gifts, offices within the church: the apostle, the prophet, the evangelist, the pastor, and the teacher. The pastor is a man or woman, not a gift. The evangelist, too, is a man or woman, and so are the apostle, the prophet, and the teacher.

Neither does this book explain what the manifestation gifts of 1 Corinthians chapter 12 are, or how they operate in the church. These gifts are generally referred to as the gifts of the Spirit. There are nine gifts in total, and they are divided into three classes: vocal (inspiration), power, and revelatory. The vocal gifts include prophesying, speaking in different kinds of tongues, and interpretation of tongues. The power gifts are the gifts of healings, working of miracles, and faith. Finally, the revelatory gifts are the word of knowledge, the word of wisdom, and discerning of spirits. These are powerful gifts for ministry, but they are not designed to help the individual believer grow in faith. Rather, they exhort, encourage, and comfort the believer.

The apostle Paul's instructions to the church for using the gifts of the Holy Spirit in a church service can be very confusing, but this book does not attempt to answer any questions arising from these instructions. The sole purpose of this book is to present the most powerful gift that God gave to man, the ability to speak to God in a supernatural language. It explains how to receive the gift and how to benefit from its use.

Introduction

Man is the only being on the earth that communicates with language. Man was made in the likeness of God, and God is a Spirit. Therefore, man is a spirit being. He has a soul and lives in a body. Angels and devils also communicate with language; they are also spirit beings. Animals do not have a spirit, so they are not spirit beings; they do not have souls like men do. Man is the only creature placed on the earth by God that communicates with language. Man is a speaking spirit.

Although much research has been conducted on "animal language," a harsh criticism of animal language studies by Dr. Herbert Terrace and others (1979) in an article published in Science, New Series Vol. 206, No. 4421 (Pages 891-902) titled, "Can an ape create a sentence"; signaled the end of the era of animal language research. In 2002, Dr. William J. Cromie, in an article titled "Research debate origin of language: Do monkeys have anything interesting to say?" published in the *Harvard Gazette* wrote, "Birds sing, chimps grunt, whales whistle, but these sounds fall short of expressing the richness of their experiences. Their lack of language goes to the question of why humans have it, but other animals do not." Animals can communicate with one another, but not through language, in the true sense of the word. Language is reserved for spirit beings.

Human language is well-defined and can theoretically be understood by any and all among a people's group. A language can be learned, and is used to communicate abstract and complex thoughts. Animals make sounds which can be understood by members of their own species, and perhaps by some other species, but they do not use language. Language sets man apart from the other creatures of the earth.

With language, we communicate our thoughts, our feelings, our actions, and our desires for ourselves and others. We use language to communicate and fellowship with God, our maker. God understands and communicates in every language that is spoken on the earth.

Satan and his demons can also communicate with mankind in every human language. Even in our private prayers to God, what we say to Him is not hidden from the Devil. He hears and understands what we want from God. But God has restored to us a new language that the Devil does not understand—this is the language from heaven.

> For then I will restore to the peoples a pure language
> that they all may call on the name of the Lord, to serve
> Him with one accord.
> —Zephaniah 3:9

Everyone who desires this can communicate with God and God alone, without Satan's interference, by using this language.

Life is full of trouble

> Man who is born of woman is of few days and full of
> trouble.
>
> —Job 14:1

Jesus said that men ought always to pray and not lose heart (Luke 18:1). This is mandatory action. Humans should pray constantly for spiritual, mental, emotional, and physical well-being. Prayer is a vital part of life on earth, and requires the use of language. Everyone should make time to pray. Many today feel pain because they have not discovered the important place of prayer. The efficacy of prayer determines our lot in life, and since all we have is what God grants us, we must pray effectively if we want God to grant us our hearts' desires.

The apostle Paul asked, "What have you that you did not receive?" (1 Corinthians 4:7). This means that God gave us everything we have. The more we can receive from God, the better our lives can be. We constantly find ourselves in need of one thing or another, and often, we feel helpless about our troubles, which can make us faint of heart, discouraged, depressed, or even suicidal. God is the only true help for these misfortunes. The only way out of trouble is to have God answer your prayers.

> Give us help from trouble, for the help of man is
> useless.
>
> —Psalm 60:11

As Christians, we must make our prayer lives effective to ensure our victory over the troubles of life. We need help from heaven! Heaven is willing to give us help, but we must be able to reach heaven to get it. Effective prayer is the only way to reach heaven. This is the system God put in place to allow man to meet his needs.

We must pray if we want to rid ourselves of the troubles of life (Psalms 34:17, 19). Other men may be able to help us, but help from men is limited. True deliverance from trouble can come only from God. The knowledge of God's word concerning prayer, and a willingness to obey is what makes the difference in a man's life.

This book endeavors to draw our attention to the power of prayer, and the great blessing that comes into our lives when we pray to God, not only with our natural language, but especially with the supernatural language that He has made available to us. Consistent and devoted use of this language in prayer should bring about dramatic change to your understanding of the kingdom of God, and help you receive more answers to your prayers. We all want our prayers answered—but how can we be sure that God hears, and that the answers to our prayers are on their way?

CHAPTER 1

THE FIRST REVELATION

Man is the crown of God's creation—at least in the world we can see. We are told that God created the universe with the word of His power. He made man in His image and placed him in the garden He planted. The fact that He created man in His image sets man apart from the rest of God's creation. All human beings—those who believe in Him and those who do not—were created in His likeness. Angels are wonderful beings, powerful and glorious, but they were not created in God's likeness. Man, on the other hand, carries God's glory. The Bible tells us that Adam was the son of God (Luke 3:38).

Revelation is the unveiling of secrets. When God divulges things that only He knows to man, these things become revelation. A fallen man has hope only in what God, in His infinite love, reveals to him. The Bible tells us that the secret knowledge belongs to the Lord our God, but what is revealed belongs to our children and to us forever (Deuteronomy 29:29). The revelations of the Scriptures are for our benefit. God's words are revelations of life's secrets to us to help us on our walk through life. Revelation from God is the key to true success in life.

Revelation of the power of words

God's greatest revelation to man was the Lord Jesus Christ, the Word of God. God's first revelation to man was the power of the spoken word. He showed us how powerful faith-filled words could be in the account of the creation of the world in Genesis.

After the heavens and the earth, God created light (Genesis 1:3). Before the creation of light, the earth was dark and without form. Therefore, the creation of light was the beginning of the creation of order. There can be no order without the presence of light. Jesus is the Light that gives light to every man coming into the world (John 1:9). Without Christ, no one can have true light nor true order in his or her life. His presence in your life signifies the beginning of order.

Revelation is light, and revelation leads to order. Receive Jesus Christ fully and let Him bring light to the dark areas of your life. Let Him bring you healing and order. Receive Him today by asking Him to come into your heart, and then enter into a lifetime of discovery! Let Him enlighten you to the truth of the Scriptures. He is the Word of God, and the Word gives light, which did not exist until God said, "Let there be light."

It is significant that light was made on the first day of creation (Genesis 1:3-4), but the Sun was created on the fourth day (Genesis 1:14-19). We are not told the nature of this light, but we know that it was not generated by the Sun. I believe it was supernatural light that preceded the creation of order and beauty. There is natural light and there is supernatural light; supernatural light precedes and has dominion over natural light. The knowledge of God is supernatural light, and it helps us live with wisdom and understanding. This leads to success in life.

The entrance of Your words gives light; it gives understanding to the simple.

—Psalm 119:130

Light and the Word of God

The word precedes light; there could be no light without the Word of God. We know that light came into the natural world through words. Spiritually, we cannot have light (revelation) without the Word of God. Revelation comes from true understanding of God's Word. Revelation is knowledge of the truth that sets us free from our troubles.

Knowledge and right understanding of God's Word come with the revelation of the blessings that are ours in Christ. Just as the words God spoke brought physical light into the world, the Word of God today brings light into dark and confused lives. God's Light is the hope and future of every man.

The Word of God is the answer to all that demonizes the human soul. It dispels darkness from the human soul, and the light that it brings fills the soul with unspeakable joy and glory (1 Peter 1:8). No one who honors the Word of God will ever be confused about life. The Word of God tells us about ourselves; it illuminates our origins and tells us where we are going. It reveals to us how to live victorious and successful lives. It is the road map of life, and our only source of light in a very dark world.

Just words

The Bible is a goldmine of all that is good. An opinion about how man should pursue a successful life must be supported by the Bible, otherwise it is just words—an empty philosophy that addresses only the symptoms of human problems rather than the causes. Any book written to help believers on their faith walks—including this one—must be fully backed by the Word of God. The Word gives light. The Bible is the entrance to God's light-giving words, and it "gives understanding to the simple" (Psalm 119:130). The opinions of men have no light unless they are backed up by the Word of God.

The Spirit of the Lord moved over the face of the waters of a world that was formless, void and dark. Then God said, "Let there be light"; and there was light (Genesis 1:1-3). The Spirit was already at work even before God spoke. Then the Spirit and the Word produced everything in creation. Words without the Spirit are just words. Jesus was the Word of God. He was God. (John 1:1).

The Word of God was conceived in Mary by the power of the Holy Spirit, who brings the Word of God into the realm of the flesh, our natural, visible world. It is the Holy Spirit who manifests the word of God in the natural realm where we can see, feel, hear, taste, or smell His work in our world (John1:14). Nothing in a Christian's life works without the Holy Spirit. We need Him more than we need air, food, or water.

The Bible is replete with Scriptures that tell us about the power of words. Even more powerful than the natural words that we speak, are words spoken supernaturally.

CHAPTER 2

LANGUAGE FROM HEAVEN

The Bible tells us in Zephaniah that God will restore to us a pure language: "For then I will restore to the peoples a pure language that they all may call on the name of the Lord, to serve Him with one accord" (Zephaniah 3:9). To restore means to reinstate, or to bring back. This Scripture implies that we have lost our own pure language. When did we lose it? I believe it was when Adam sinned and took on the nature of Satan. He was still a creature of God, but a son of Satan. Jesus said to some people, "You are of your father the Devil" (John 8:44). Adam's nature changed the day he sinned, and I believe he lost the "pure language" he used to communicate with God.

It is interesting to note that all one hundred and twenty disciples of Jesus were with one accord in one place when the Holy Spirit came from heaven on the day of Pentecost (Acts 2:1-4). They all received their new language from heaven on that day.

Christ's redemptive work is the restoration of all things. A vital part of this is the restoration of a new tongue with which to call upon God and serve Him with one accord. I believe the language referred to in Zephaniah is the ability to speak with other tongues. This is the language with which to communicate and fellowship fully with God. It is the language of our born-again spirit—and we must worship God not only in truth, but also in spirit (John 4:24). Some call speaking in tongues our prayer language.

The prayer language

God, in His infinite wisdom, gave us a way to pray effectively by giving us a prayer language to guarantee that it is His will which we pray for and accomplish in our lives. The Bible tells us that we do not know what we should pray for as we ought, but the Spirit prays for us according to the will of God (Romans 8:26-27).

Jesus promised to bless us with His Spirit after He has gone to be with His Father in heaven. The Bible calls the Spirit "the Promise of the Father" in Acts 1:4. The Holy Spirit is also called "the Helper" in John 14:16. We can only draw near to God with the help of the Holy Spirit. We must not allow fear, misunderstanding, or teachings against the Holy Spirit to prevent us from seeking God. Speaking in tongues is of God; God gave us the ability because he wants us to pray to Him in tongues.

Some believe speaking in tongues is of the Devil, but this is not true. Many Christians around the world, possibly millions, pray in tongues and love God. They speak in tongues to worship Jesus as their Lord and Savior. The gift they have received is definitely not from the Devil; if the Devil is in a man, he does not allow the man to worship or honor the name of Jesus. The supernatural ability to speak in tongues must be from God. Why would any Christian shy away from receiving this gift from God? Truly, it is the Devil who wants God's people to believe that speaking in tongues is something to be feared. By deceiving them in this way, he prevents them from reaching out to God for the gift, thus hindering them from reaching their full potential in Christ. Jesus said that anyone who attributes the Holy Spirit's work to the Devil blasphemes the Holy Spirit, and sin against the Holy Spirit is unpardonable, never forgiven (Mark 3:28-30).

Speaking in tongues is a supernatural act. If Jesus' own disciples needed the Holy Spirit and the ability to speak in tongues to help them with their faith, then we today must certainly need the Holy Spirit too. Knowledge of the truth brings us freedom.

Christians have spoken in tongues ever since the New Testament began. We are still living in the days of the New Testament; it has not yet come to an end, and Jesus is still our Lord. "Jesus Christ is the same yesterday, today, and forever" (Hebrews 13:8). Speaking in tongues is still a tool for us to use today. We must never be afraid of what God has given to us. This book will use quotations from the Scriptures to show you why it is the express will of God that all believers speak in tongues. If you do not yet understand this truth, then you must pray with an open mind. God is sure to reveal the truth to you if you go to Him with humility and a sincere desire to know. If we seek, we will find. If we cry out to God with hearts hungry for God, God will reveal Himself. He will not leave us in the dark, confused and not knowing what to do.

A Christian who can speak in tongues isn't any more a child of God than a Christian who can't. Everyone who receives Christ as Lord and Savior is born again and will be with Jesus in heaven. However, a believer must strive to use all that God offers us in this life to become a better servant of the Lord on earth. We must hunger and thirst for righteousness (Matthew 5:6).

You might be a great servant of God at the moment, but with more of the Holy Spirit in your life, you could be even better. The

Holy Spirit makes us what we are in God. When the disciples needed boldness to speak God's word with power, He gave them more of the Holy Spirit (Acts 4:23-31). God answers our need for the power to do His will by anointing us with the Holy Spirit. This book offers a key tool of God's, speaking in tongues, that will make a big difference in our service to God here on earth.

Every time we speak with tongues, something supernatural is happening. Speaking in tongues is a supernatural act. It is hard to explain or to understand, but the supernatural is right there! Speaking in tongues is a miracle, a supernatural language spoken effortlessly with the help of the Holy Spirit in us. God, in His love, is helping us to communicate more effectively with Him so that our spirits can truly know Him. "For he who speaks in a tongue does not speak to men but to God, for no one understands him; however, in the spirit he speaks mysteries" (1 Corinthians 14:2).

Man was created in God's image to be able to fellowship with God. No other being in the whole of creation can do that. We can commune with one another, but we are not meant to be satisfied by fellowship with other men; it doesn't meet the needs of our being. We need communion with God. It is also possible to have some form of fellowship with animals, but God knew that would not be good enough for Adam; He gave him Eve, one of his own kind. It is difficult for us to have lost our full ability to communicate with God, but God has restored to us a means to communicate with Him through His Spirit.

God created the Angels and all the heavenly beings, but none were created in His image. God can only find full communion with man, who was created in His likeness. We need true fellowship with God, and there is no better way to achieve it than to speak to God in the supernatural language of tongues (1 Corinthians 14:14-15).

The words of Adam, the son of God (Luke 3:38), had power, just like those of His Creator. Adam gave names to all the animals that God created. "Out of the ground the Lord God formed every beast of the field and every bird of the air, and brought them to Adam to see what he would call them. And whatever Adam called each living creature, that was its name" (Genesis 2:19). Adam had dominion, which he expressed through his words.

Adam was made in God's very image. He could fellowship with God. But after the fall, things were different for Adam. His nature changed. He could no longer effectively communicate with the source of his life. He was not comfortable in God's presence. He would rather hide.

His knowledge was different after he had sinned. Through sinning, he received knowledge of good and evil that destroyed his pure spirit. After the fall, his new language carried death with it rather than just life (Proverb 18:21). God's words give life. In man's fallen state, words of death are spoken often. The redemptive work of our Lord Jesus ushers in the born-again spirit (2 Corinthians 5:17). We must now learn to speak words that bring life rather than words that bring death. We can do all things through Christ, who strengthens us (Philippians 4:13).

Our new nature is able to communicate with our maker. God restored to us the ability to speak with a pure tongue (Zephaniah 3:9) along with the restoration of the dominion He intended when He initially put man on the earth.

The gift of the Holy Spirit injects more life than death into our words, and it will inject more of the nature of God into us. As we increase our communication in tongues, His divine power flows into our lives. On the day of Pentecost, all who believed and waited for the coming of the Spirit received Him; they all ended up speaking in tongues (Acts 2:2-4). This is one of the signs Jesus told us would follow those who believe in Him (Mark 16:15-18). Every believer has the right to have this sign in his or her life, too. Believers today who welcome the Holy Spirit will also speak in tongues. Jesus sent Him to be with us until the end of the age. He is here for a purpose. He has work to do in us.

> And these signs will follow those who believe: In My name they will cast out demons; they will speak with new tongues.
>
> —Mark 16:17

CHAPTER 3

THE POWER OF LANGUAGE

Language is for communication

Many people have rejected Christ, our Redeemer and King, and giver of this new heavenly language. Some who have accepted Christ have rejected the gift. People may reject the precious gift of speaking in tongues due to past teachings that may have been based on man's ideas and feelings, and on what others said. God gave us language to communicate not only with one another, but also with Him.

Effective communication is associated with power. Our ability to work together depends heavily on our ability to communicate effectively with one another. I believe that greater power is available to us when we are able to effectively communicate with God. In the workplace, a breakdown in communication diminishes productivity. We can release more of God's power into our lives by effectively communicating with Him using the language from heaven. God is a Spirit; He seeks those who will worship Him in spirit and truth (John 4:24).

Ruled by the physical senses

Human language allows us to communicate naturally with our fellow man. In addition to our natural language, we need a spirit language to effectively communicate with God. Before the fall, man was more of a spirit being than a natural being. He was made in the image of God. After the fall, however, he became more of a natural being ruled by the physical senses. His spirit took on another nature, one foreign to God. This new language from heaven—the ability to speak with other tongues—fully restores man's ability to communicate with God in the realm of the spirit, bypassing his natural senses. Even the Devil cannot understand what is being communicated. Only God does. "For he who speaks in a tongue does not speak to men but to God, for no one understands him; however, in the spirit he speaks mysteries" (1 Corinthians 14:2). This wonderful gift is a privilege from God to man—we should not neglect it.

The power of one language

People who speak the same language are able to communicate ideas, thoughts, and emotions with one another. The Bible tells us that at one time, everyone in the world spoke the same language. They were all together in one place. The people of the world then decided to build a tower to reach up to the heavens. This was contrary to the will of God.

> And the Lord said, "Indeed the people are one and they all have one language, and this is what they begin to do; now nothing that they propose to do will be

withheld from them. Come, let Us go down and there confuse their language, that they may not understand one another's speech."

—Genesis 11:6-7

When the people shared one language, they were as one. Unity provides power, even the power to do evil. Their unity had great power. God said that nothing they proposed to do would be withheld from them. In order words, nothing that they set their hearts to do would be impossible. The only way to stop the building of the tower was to bring confusion into their language. It was not God's will for them to build the tower. God wanted them to spread out and cover the face of the earth, but they were more comfortable staying together in one place. God used language to fulfill His will and force mankind to fill the earth.

In the book of Acts, Christ's followers were in one accord waiting for God on the day of Pentecost. They were not rebelling against His will. After He rose from the dead, Jesus had told them not to depart from Jerusalem, but to wait for the promise of the Father. Finally, the Holy Spirit came and filled them, and they began to speak in other tongues as the Spirit gave utterance (Acts 1:4). The purpose of this was again to spread them out into the world with the Word of God. They were to be witnesses in Jerusalem, Judea, and Samaria (Acts 1:8). They were to spread these new languages from heaven to the ends of the earth by preaching the gospel. Everyone who believed and received Christ could then receive the baptism of the Holy Spirit and speak in other tongues.

When the people who listened to Peter's preaching on the day of Pentecost asked, "Men and brethren what shall we do?" Peter replied, "Repent, and let every one of you be baptized in the name of Jesus Christ for the remission of sins; and you shall receive the gift of the Holy Spirit" (Acts 2:38). Peter said the promise of the Holy Spirit was for those who heard him preach, their children, and for those who were far off. This included all believers. Peter said if they believed and repented they would receive the Holy Spirit. How would they receive the promise of the Holy Spirit? In the same way Peter and the other disciples had: with speaking in tongues. In other words, God wanted these new languages from heaven spread around the world.

God used language to scatter mankind around the globe in order to make man seek Him. Today, he uses speaking in tongues to draw mankind closer to Himself and to help them seek Him in unity.

> And He has made from one blood every nation of men
> to dwell on all the face of the earth, and has determined
> their pre-appointed times and the boundaries of their
> dwellings, so that they should seek the Lord, in the
> hope that they might grope for Him and find Him,
> though He is not far from each one of us.
>
> —Acts 17:26-27

Not only does speaking in tongues open up better communication with God, it also brings greater unity. If believers all over the world spent more prayer time speaking in tongues, the language of our born-again spirit (1 Corinthians 14:14), the world would experience more of the presence of God, and peace would exist on the earth. The eminent will of God would result in love, peace, joy, and unity among men.

> For with stammering lips and another tongue He will
> speak to this people, To whom He said, "This is the

rest with which You may cause the weary to rest," And,
"This is the refreshing."

—Isaiah 28:11-12

Our natural language is limited

When we have one language and one speech with God, we become as one with Him. Nothing can be withheld from us as we seek to do His will. If only the whole church world had one language and one speech! A greater power would be available to us in His name, and nothing would be impossible. Thank God that in His infinite wisdom, He has made it possible for us to effectively communicate with Him through the power of the Holy Spirit. On the day of Pentecost, the Holy Spirit was given to us, and with His coming, the birth of a new language. This is a spirit-language. This is the pure language that God promised to restore to us: speaking in tongues. God said: "For then I will restore to the peoples a pure language that they all may call on the name of the Lord, to serve Him with one accord" (Zephaniah 3:9).

The restored language is our prayer language. We call on God with this language and He hears and understands what we are saying from the core of our being, from our hearts. We do not have to learn this new language; it has been given to us. Our native tongue is of the flesh. God can communicate with us through our native tongue, but the flesh gets in the way; our selfish desires are expressed more loudly when we pray in our fleshly language. This form of communication between God and man is limited. Jesus said, "God is Spirit, and those who worship Him must worship Him in spirit and in truth" (John 4:24). We do not always pray according to His will in our natural language. But when we pray in our spirit's language, our selfish desires are not communicated. The desires of our heart, of our born-again spirit, are communicated (Romans 8:26-27). Speaking in other tongues brings our communication with God to its absolute fullest. Scripturally, it is the only way to communicate with God effectively. Every believer has this privilege.

> For he who speaks in a tongue does not speak to men but to God, for no one understands him; however, in the spirit he speaks mysteries.
> —1 Corinthians 14:2

Notice the Word of God says that we worship Him not only in spirit, but in truth, also. The Word of God is truth (John 17:17). Everything we do in word or deed must line up with God's Word. Many people say, "Everyone has his or her own interpretation of the truth from God's Word." This opinion may have an element of truth to it, but one sincerely seeking to know the truth and to know God should be guided by the Holy Spirit.

A given truth or principle of God's Word is always supported by several Scriptures from the pages of the Bible. God usually confirms His Word with signs (Mark 16:20). We must not accept a principle from God's Word based on only one passage from the Bible. The Bible has a way of weaving the threads of truth around a given principle. Speaking in tongues is one such truth. Jesus said, "It is the spirit that gives life, the flesh profits nothing" (John 6:63).

To live a life pleasing to God is to live a life in the Spirit. The Word of God gives us light or insight into truth. A hungry heart searches for truth, and God does not disappoint. Likewise, a heart unwilling to live according to God's truth is hardened by choice so that the Word of God cannot accomplish its purpose. God allows mankind choices, but each choice is followed by consequence: a blessing or a curse. It is not wise to dismiss truth from the Word of God as irrelevant without a true desire to search for light and understanding, the truth of the Scriptures. Jesus said that the words He spoke to us would be our judge on judgment day (John 12:48). But judgment is already here.

> He who believes in Him is not condemned; but he who does not believe is condemned already, because he has not believed in the name of the only begotten Son of God.
>
> —John 3:18

CHAPTER 4

TONGUES ARE ONLY FOR NEW TESTAMENT BELIEVERS

God performed great miracles in the Old Testament, as well as the New Testament. The Spirit of God came to the judges, the priests, the prophets, and the kings of the Old Testament. God used them mightily, but none of the Old Testament saints spoke in tongues. The new language from heaven is for New Testament people. No one could speak in this heavenly language if not for the new birth, which became available to mankind after the death and resurrection of the Lord Jesus Christ. Only the re-born spirit of man can receive this new language.

> I will give you a new heart and put a new spirit within you; I will take the heart of stone out of your flesh and give you a heart of flesh. I will put My Spirit within you and cause you to walk in My statutes, and you will keep My judgments and do them.
>
> —Ezekiel 36:26-27

Jesus said, "The Spirit of truth, whom the world cannot receive, because it neither sees Him nor knows Him; but you know Him, for He dwells with you and will be in you" (John 14:17). Here, Jesus is saying that the unsaved world cannot receive the Spirit of God. You do not put new wine into an old wine skin, but new wine into new wine skins (Matthew 9:17). The Holy Spirit is given only to those who have been born again—those with a new wine skin. The born-again experience creates a new wine skin for the Holy Spirit to be poured into.

No Old Testament saint spoke in tongues. John the Baptist was of the Old Testament, and although he was filled with the Holy Spirit from his mother's womb, he did not speak in tongues (Luke 1:15). John was the last prophet of the Old Testament. Jesus never spoke in tongues. The Bible tells us that in the fullness of time, God sent forth His Son, born of a woman, born under the law (Galatians 4:4). Jesus and John were born under the law. Jesus ushered in the New Testament and the born-again experience through His sacrificial death. Jesus did not need to speak in tongues. His spirit was the Spirit of God. He never had the sinful nature. His Spirit did not need the new birth to communicate effectively with the Father—but our spirits do.

No one in the Old Testament spoke in tongues, not even Jesus. No one could, even if they knew about the gift and wanted to speak in tongues. Speaking in tongues was not available to any in the Old Testament. It was not a part of Old Testament worship and service to God. However, speaking in tongues is a part of New Testament worship and service to God, and is available to every believer in the New Testament. Thus, every believer under the New Testament, who wants, can speak in tongues.

Joel's prophecy

God promised mankind a new spirit and a new heart. He also promised that He would put His Spirit into man (Ezekiel 36:26-27). The prophet Joel, however, went a little further by telling us when this would happen, and what will follow the outpouring of the Holy Spirit.

> But this is what was spoken by the prophet Joel: And it shall come to pass in the last days, says God, that I will pour out of My Spirit on all flesh; your sons and your daughters shall prophesy, your young men shall see visions, your old men shall dream dreams.
>
> —Acts 2:16-17

With the fulfillment of Joel's prophecy, another language with which to communicate with God and express His glory was introduced to mankind. This new supernatural language connects the spirit of man directly to God in unfiltered communication. It is prayer from man aided by the Spirit of God, prayer of the spirit of man in union with the Spirit of God. It gives the man divine power and authority to operate in the realm of spirits, or the unseen world, and divine peace as the Prince of Peace takes control of the most powerful organ member of a man's body.

> Death and life are in the power of the tongue, and those who love it will eat its fruit.
>
> —Proverbs 18:21

The power of the tongue

Early in the creation account, God revealed the power of spoken words. The Bible tells us that one who does not stumble in what he says is a perfect man with control over his whole body (James 3:2). James tells us that control over the body is tied to control of the tongue, and that the tongue is like a bit in a horse's mouth. The rider uses it to control its movements. James also tells us that the tongue is like the rudder of a ship that the captain uses to steer the ship in the direction he wishes to go.

> Indeed, we put bits in horses' mouths that they may obey us, and we turn their whole body. Look also at ships: although they are so large and are driven by fierce winds they are turned by a very small rudder wherever the pilot desires. Even so the tongue is a little member and boasts great things.
>
> —James 3:3-5

James seems to suggest that the tongue holds the key to our destiny. Our tongues determine our destiny. The tongue determines where we wind up in life. What comes out of our mouths in words is so powerful that Jesus said that on judgment day, we must give account of every idle word we have spoken. In other words, Jesus is saying no word is meaningless. Once spoken, it goes into action, healing or making sick, giving life or causing death. We will give an account of our words because they do something to us and to others.

> But I say to you that for every idle word men may speak, they will give account of it in the Day of Judgment. For

by your words you will be justified, and by your words
you will be condemned.

—Matthew 12:36-37

Words are powerful! The words of our mouths bring freedom or
bondage, give justification or condemnation—we have the choice
of which words to speak. The Bible tells us it is with the heart
that a man believes and is made righteous before God, but it is his
confession of Jesus Christ as Savior that brings salvation (Romans
10:10). In other words, a man cannot enjoy the benefits of God's
righteousness until he uses his mouth.

Salvation will not come from believing with one's heart alone.
Open confession of faith in Christ is what brings the power of
salvation into one's life. The righteousness that a man gains from
having belief in his heart will do him no good in the natural world
unless he is willing to use his mouth to confess what he believes.
This is why it is not wise to be a "closet Christian." A closet
Christian is powerless, and his life will reflect that. Those who
speak of faith in Christ fearlessly and openly live more powerful
lives in Christ. Many Christians do not yet fully understand the
power of their words. Jesus left us with His words. Through the
power of the Holy Spirit, they are changing lives.

> But what does it say? "The word is near you, in your
> mouth and in your heart" (that is, the word of faith
> which we preach): that if you confess with your mouth
> the Lord Jesus and believe in your heart that God has
> raised Him from the dead, you will be saved. For with
> the heart one believes unto righteousness, and with the
> mouth confession is made unto salvation.
>
> —Romans 10:8-10

The Bible tells us that faith comes through hearing of the Word of God (Romans 10:17). When we hear the Word preached in faith, it gets into our hearts and gives birth to faith. As soon as faith has been born in our hearts, our mouths are ready to speak. This is the natural process for the spirit of faith.

> And since we have the same spirit of faith, according to what is written, "I believed and therefore I spoke," we also believe and therefore speak.
> —2 Corinthians 4:13

If there is genuine faith in the heart, the mouth will speak. Notice the Bible tells us that one believes with the heart and is made righteous before God. Righteousness is a gift. By grace through faith, we are saved. Our own works never bring us salvation (Ephesians 2:8-9).

What we say with our mouths matters. "Salvation" comes from the Greek word "sozo," meaning to be healed, preserved, or rescued, to be made whole, or to do well. A man may be righteous before God on the inside, but his righteousness will not affect his life until he begins to speak openly about his faith. Words are very powerful! This is why I believe God gave us this revelation very early in Genesis, in the account of creation. God said, "Let there be light, and there was light" (Genesis 1:3). God wants us to know that words spoken by spirit beings are powerful; they come to pass. Light does not exist until the words "Let there be light" are spoken.

If what we say affects our lives, then what happens when we speak in tongues with the aid of God's Holy Spirit? We speak words that are powerful and undefiled. We speak words that God intended for us to speak. We speak God's words. There is no

doubt that speaking the Spirit's words changes our lives and our world. If we speak with the help of the Spirit, we are not speaking natural words, but supernatural ones. If the Holy Spirit guides the words, then the words spoken must be God's, and if they are God's words, then faith will grow in our hearts. The Word of God is the carrier of faith. No wonder St. Jude told us to strengthen our faith through praying in the Spirit, or speaking in tongues: "But you, beloved, building yourselves up on your most holy faith, praying in the Holy Spirit" (Jude 1:20).

If praying in the Spirit builds or strengthens one's faith, what would happen to a believer who spends at least an hour each day praying in tongues? What would happen to a church if the pastor called for all members to spend a night praying to God in one accord, in tongues? The faith of these believers would shoot up to the heavens, and miracles would begin to take place in their midst! They would quickly find that God truly can meet all their needs, and their church would be a vibrant, people-loving, soul-seeking church. Through faith born of praying in tongues, every child of God can find true freedom in life. Jesus' words, "if the Son makes you free, you will be free indeed," then become a living reality by the power of the Spirit (John 8:36).

CHAPTER 5

WORDS ARE SEED

Words are seed, and when sown or spoken, they produce fruit. Thoughts can go through our heads, but if we do not speak or act on them, they die a natural death. If they are not sown, they cannot bear fruit. Jesus said, "the seed is the Word of God" (Luke 8:11). Our words are also seeds, but the Word of God is an incorruptible seed (1 Peter 1:23).

> A man's stomach shall be satisfied from the fruit of his mouth; from the produce of his lips he shall be filled. Death and life are in the power of the tongue, and those who love it will eat its fruit.
>
> —Proverbs 18:20-21

What the above passage is telling us is that words affect our lives. If your words are wholesome, your belly will be satisfied, and you will be successful. However, if your words are defiled, negative, and filled with doubt, you will suffer want. The Word of God tells us that death and life are inherent in our words. There is either death or life—there cannot be both at the same time. If we speak from the Word of God, wholesomely, positively, and faithfully, we revive, and things in our lives that were dying come back to life. Accordingly, when we speak words of death, life declines and the good things in our life begin to die.

God revealed to us that our words do things that cannot be observed with our natural senses. However, in time, their effects become evident. When the captain of a large ship turns the ship in the direction he has chosen, for a while, it will seem the ship is not doing what the captain wants. However, in time, it will become evident that the ship, huge as it is, must obey the "words" coming from the little rudder (the tongue). Now think about this: if what we say with our mouths affects our lives for good or bad depending on what we are saying, what do you think would happen if we often talked in the supernatural language of tongues? We would still use our tongues, but the words spoken would be heavenly. I believe the words we speak in the Spirit, in tongues, can bring us heaven on earth.

The parable of the sower

In the parable of the sower, a sower scatters seeds on the wayside, on the stony, the thorny, and the good ground. Jesus refers to the seeds sown as the Word of God (Luke 8:11). Our words are also seeds; they produce for us what we say. What comes out of our mouths can bring us life or death. When we speak in tongues, we are still using our own tongues with the power of life and death in them, but we have taken our words to a divine level with the help of the Holy Spirit. There is no doubt that this practice will bring much supernatural life into our beings. The words we speak in tongues are supernatural seeds yielding supernatural fruit in our lives, some a hundredfold, some sixty, some thirty (Matthew 13:23).

Rest for those who believe

In both the Old and New Testaments, God spoke much about entering into rest and finding rest for our souls. Rest is something God considers very beneficial for man. No one can function without some rest. How do we find true rest? Certainly, we find rest in Jesus Christ, but let us consider the Scriptural passage below.

> For with stammering lips and another tongue He will speak to this people, to whom He said, "This is the rest with which You may cause the weary to rest," And, "This is the refreshing"; Yet they would not hear. But the word of the Lord was to them, "Precept upon precept, precept upon precept, line upon line, line upon line, here a little, there a little," That they might go and fall backward, and be broken and snared and caught.
>
> —Isaiah 28:11-13

Stammering lips here refers to speaking in tongues (1 Corinthians 14:21). In this passage in Isaiah, God tells us that this is the rest with which God will cause the weary to rest. Speaking in tongues brings us rest; this is the refreshing the Word of God speaks about.

Multiple times in my life, an event has taken place which troubled me and caused me to lose my peace. Fear came in like wildfire to devour me. Hope seemed lost, but by just spending a few minutes every day speaking to God in tongues, my hope was restored, and with it, peace, rest, and deliverance.

Many Christians today are wearied by the troubles of life. They work hard to take care of one problem, but as soon as it is resolved, another comes up. Instead of going to God in prayer, many spend time talking to others about their problems, seeking solutions from men. The result is that they cannot enter into rest. The Bible says, "Give us help from trouble, for the help of man is useless" (Psalm 60:11). Speaking in tongues is the answer for resting the soul. Speaking in tongues brings refreshing to the weary.

The Bible tells us that a true worshiper worships the Father in spirit and truth (John 4:23). It is good to worship the Father in truth, but we must also worship in spirit. According to Isaiah the prophet, without the Spirit, following the Word leads to a religious life devoid of power, joy, and peace. Isaiah says believers will go and fall backward and be broken (Isaiah 28:11-13). It is not enough to live by precept upon precept from the Scriptures. Progress cannot be made from such exercise alone. Not by might nor by power, but by the Spirit is progress made (Zechariah 4:6).

It is the Spirit who gives life; the flesh profits nothing (John 6:63). Speaking in tongues helps us with our desire to worship the Father in spirit and in truth. The Holy Spirit teaches us the truth and helps us to be spiritual in our day-to-day living. Many times, we just need refreshing. True refreshing only comes through praying in other tongues before God. One can stay revived if he or she commits to praying in tongues daily for prolonged periods of time. This is like keeping your battery constantly charged. Many Christians talk about the refreshing the Word of God speaks about, but do not know how to find it. Speaking in tongues is one sure way to find refreshing in God. If you need revival in your life, spend time praying in tongues.

We do not know what to pray for

As mere humans, and not God, we are unable to know things we don't perceive with all or some of our five senses. The Bible considers this a form of weakness on our part with regards to effective prayer (Romans 8:26). A son or daughter may be returning home on the same road that a drunk driver is taking to get home. There is a strong potential for mishap. However, we are unaware of the potential for trouble. How does a parent know what to pray for concerning his or her child in a situation like the one described above? Yet God wants us to be specific when we pray and ask Him for things.

Jesus said to the blind man who was crying out to Him for mercy, "What do you want me to do for you?" (Mark 10:51). Everyone around knew that the blind man wanted his eyes opened. His need was obvious to all, but Jesus still wanted him to voice what he wanted from God.

God wants us to be specific in our requests, but how do we accurately pray in situations we know nothing about? We are rarely aware when something bad is taking place or about to take place. If we did know, we would cry out to God for help, but most of the time we are clueless. We have no knowledge. It is beyond us to know. We cannot pray for what we know nothing about. And if we do pray, we cannot address the problem to God specifically. This is why the Bible tells us that we do not know what to pray for. Note that the Bible does not say we do not know how to pray. The problem is knowing exactly what to pray for. Knowing what to pray for has a lot to do with getting our prayers answered. But, thank God, the Holy Spirit is here to help us with this weakness.

> Likewise the Spirit also helps in our weaknesses.
> For we do not know what we should pray for as we

ought, but the Spirit Himself makes intercession for
us with groaning's which cannot be uttered. Now He
who searches the hearts knows what the mind of the
Spirit is, because He makes intercession for the saints
according to the will of God.

—Romans 8:26-27

We most need the Holy Spirit's help in prayers of intercession.
There are different kinds of prayer—prayers for forgiveness of
sin, prayers of dedication, spiritual warfare in prayer, prayers of
supplication. In these types of prayer, we know for the most part
what we want from God. In prayers of intercession, however, when
we are praying for someone else, we may not know exactly what to
pray for. We need the Holy Spirit to help intercede for us.

The Holy Spirit is God. He knows all things. He prays
specifically for us and through us according to God's will for us
and for the lives of our loved ones. In His intercession, He bypasses
our minds as He makes requests to the Father on our behalf.
He does so by speaking through us in tongues. He bypasses the
natural mind, which does not know the danger that the Devil has
planned for our child who is returning home from visiting a friend.
The Devil may have placed a drunk driver on the same path to
accomplish his evil plan. However, God, who knows all things,
moves in us through His Holy Spirit, who prays inside us and
nullifies Satan's plan.

The Bible tells us, "For as many as are led by the Spirit of God,
these are the sons of God" (Romans 8:14). The Spirit always prays
through us to God according to the will of God. God's will for our
lives is always good.

When angels announced the birth of Christ, they sang praises
to God, saying, "Glory to God in the highest, and on earth peace,

goodwill toward men!" (Luke 2:14) God wishes goodwill to every person, never ill will. God gave us His Son so we could experience His goodwill on earth. The Holy Spirit distributes God's goodwill to man. But the Spirit needs to be in a man or woman to accomplish His work on the earth. A man with the Spirit's language inside him possesses the ability to bring heaven to earth by praying in tongues.

> So I sought for a man among them who would make a wall, and stand in the gap before Me on behalf of the land, that I should not destroy it; but, I found no one.
>
> —Ezekiel 22:30

I spent the whole of 1988 in Nigeria, my native country, ministering even though I was not in full-time ministry. A number of churches invited me to speak. One of them was a large Baptist church in the town where I grew up. The young people in that church felt they needed more of God, and had heard that I could help them receive the Holy Spirit with the evidence of speaking in tongues. I spoke to them about the Holy Spirit and prayed for those who wanted to receive. About nineteen people received that day, including a couple who might have done so previously but been unsure of what they had received; perhaps because they had not received proper instruction.

A few weeks later, I got up one morning feeling very alienated from God. It was the same kind of feeling I had just before I was saved, a feeling of being very lost. I prayed for about an hour, mostly in tongues, but I felt no release. I confessed whatever I thought I might have done wrong, but still did not feel better.

By early afternoon, the bad feelings had left, and my peace had returned. Then, a young man showed up. He was one of the

Baptist youths who had not come up to receive the Holy Spirit. He announced that he wanted to receive the Holy Spirit now. I said, "Great!" We went into my room to pray, but as soon as we got there, he said, "Sir, I have this problem that I would like you to know about before you pray." He went on to tell me that years before, he had lived a very clean life before God, but then he had made friends with the wrong kind of people. His friends had persuaded him to be with a prostitute. He said his life had changed from that day on. He could not stop himself from committing fornication. He wanted to change, but he did not think he was worthy to receive the Holy Spirit.

I then realized that I had actually been praying for this young man all morning. I told him that a demon spirit was involved and that I was going to get the demon out his life. I spoke to the demon and it manifested in a lewd way, then left him. We then prayed together for him to receive the Holy Spirit. Shortly after that, he began to speak in tongues. I understand he married and is still living as a Christian man today. To God be the glory!

The Holy Spirit helps us when we do not know what to pray for. He prayed through me for that young man who was in darkness seeking a way out because it was my practice to pray in tongues for myself and for those He has placed in my life. It was easy to free the young man of the demon that had oppressed him for years. It took only a few minutes because the Holy Spirit had already dealt with his problem before he arrived for prayer.

The authority to operate on earth

Jesus encouraged us to pray like this: "Our Father in heaven, hallowed be Your name. Your kingdom come. Your will be done

on earth as it is in heaven" (Matthew 6:8-10). In heaven, where God's will reigns supreme, no one gets sick, no one is ever broke or in debt, no one wants for anything, no one is fearful, and no one ever feels depressed or doubtful about the future.

Through this new language, the Holy Spirit can help us pray heaven down to the earth. Unless the lips of a man on earth call for God's will to be done on the earth, He will not do anything. God needs a man to work out His will on the earth. This is why, during His earthly ministry, Jesus referred to Himself more as the Son of man than as the Son of God. He was saying, "I am a true man and have the right to operate on the earth."

> The heaven, even the heavens are the Lord's; but the earth He has given to the children of men.
>
> —Psalm 115:16

This is our domain. God gave it to us. We have the right to operate here. The Devil also needs a man to carry out his evil plans on the earth. He is limited in what he can do on the earth without one. This is why he needs a man to be the Antichrist before the end of the age. Man's sin gave authority to the devil to operate on the earth. God needs a man to cooperate with Him so He can accomplish His purposes on the earth. When we ask Him to come into our lives, He does so. He uses us greatly to make life much better for us and for other humans. God is constantly looking for a man or a woman through whom He may perform His wonders on the earth, but most of us are too busy with our own lives to notice or heed His call.

God reserves the right to judge the world, but to do us good, He needs a man to agree with Him and to work with Him. God declared: "So I sought for a man among them who would make a wall, and stand in the gap before Me on behalf of the land, that I should not destroy it; but I found no one" (Ezekiel 22:30).

But He found that man in His Son Jesus. Jesus found us, and now we must cooperate with Him so that God's purposes can be accomplished. Jesus said if two people on the earth could agree on anything that they wanted from the Father, it would be done (Matthew 18:19). The two people have to be on the earth; they must be in total agreement on what they want from the Father, and they must ask. This is what it takes for the Father to bless us.

Jesus assured us that if we ask for something to be done, God, His Father, will do it. Whatever we ask of the Father in His name, the Father will give to us. How powerful it would be if we actually ask God to do something for us that He Himself wants done.

God has always wanted the best for every human, even though we may not realize it because we are too busy pursuing things that may hurt us. The Holy Spirit knows God's perfect plan. Praying in tongues moves God and our hearts to connect with the same desire, and that desire will be fulfilled on earth. This is what happens when humans ask for the perfect will of God to be done in their lives and in the world, when they pray to God in tongues.

> Now, He who searches the hearts knows what the mind of the Spirit is, because He makes intercession for the saints according to the will of God.
> —Romans 8:27

Anointed with the Holy Spirit for work

Jesus was anointed with the Holy Spirit and then went about doing good by healing all who were oppressed by the Devil (Acts 10:38).

The Holy Spirit anointed Jesus before He went out to fulfill His ministry. John the Baptist was filled with the Holy Spirit from his mother's womb (Luke 1:15). Everyone who worked for God in biblical times had the Holy Spirit come into him or her before going out to minister. We cannot do holy work without the Holy Spirit. Immediately after His baptism by John, the Holy Spirit filled Jesus.

Jesus went to John to be baptized. John did not think it was the right thing to do; he thought Jesus should baptize him. Jesus persuaded John to baptize Him to fulfill all righteousness. Jesus was baptized, and as He rose out of the water, the Holy Spirit came to Him in the form of a dove, and then a voice came from heaven. The voice was the Father announcing that He was well pleased with the Son (Matthew 3:13-17).

The Holy Spirit did not come to the Son until after the Son had done His part to fulfill all righteousness. The Father did not speak until the Holy Spirit had come to the Son. We need only do what God has told us to receive His blessings. We cannot go by our own understanding or by how we feel.

If John the Baptist needed to be filled with the Holy Spirit to live and do the work the Father called him to do, then so do we. If Jesus, the Son of God, who was without sin, needed to be filled with the Holy Spirit to do the work God gave Him to do, then so do we. If the disciples needed to be filled with the Holy Spirit to live and work for God, then we do, too. God does not change. He said, "I am the Lord, I change not" (Malachi 3:6).

Jesus had the fullness of the Holy Spirit (John 3:34). He was already the Son of God before the Holy Spirit came to Him. The Holy Spirit will not come in baptism to anyone who is not a son or daughter of God. Every born-again person must to be filled with the Holy Spirit to fulfill all righteousness. This anointing of the Holy Spirit enabled Jesus to do good and heal all who were oppressed by the Devil (Acts 10:38).

After Jesus rose from the dead, He appeared to His disciples several times. Before He was taken up into heaven, He had a good talk with them. They were eager to take over the world, but Jesus wanted them to stay in Jerusalem and wait for the promise of the Father—the Holy Spirit's baptism on the day of Pentecost. They were already born again. They were children of the Most High, but they needed the Holy Spirit, just as Jesus had, in order to live and work for God. We are still living in the era of the New Testament; we still need the Holy Spirit, as the disciples needed Him in biblical times.

CHAPTER 6

THE HOLY SPIRIT'S BAPTISM IS NOT THE SAME AS RECEIVING JESUS

Some believe that when one receives Jesus as personal Savior, he or she is baptized with the Holy Spirit at the same time. However, the Scriptures do not support this position. There is no doubt that a new spirit is created in a man or woman who receives Christ; this is the work of the Holy Spirit. When the word of faith is spoken and the hearer receives it, faith in Christ results. With faith in Christ, a new creature is born spiritually. The Bible tells us that if anyone is in Christ, he is a new creation (2 Corinthians 5:17). Chapter 36 of Ezekiel describes the new birth experience.

> I will give you a new heart and put a new spirit within you; I will take the heart of stone out of your flesh and give you a heart of flesh. I will put My Spirit within you

and cause you to walk in My statutes, and you will keep
My judgments and do them.

—Ezekiel 36:26-27

The passage says that God will give a new heart and a new spirit.
This is the new creature that 2 Corinthians 5:17 refers to: a new
creation with a new heart and a new spirit, the real you. The word
"spirit" is lowercased, meaning that it refers to the human spirit.
The stony heart and the old spirit are taken out at the new birth,
and the redemptive work of the cross puts them to death. God
said that He would then put His Spirit within the believer. God's
Spirit entering the believer is a different work from God giving
the believer a new heart and a new spirit. The new believer receives
the Holy Spirit as help for his new spirit. The Spirit of God in
the new believer causes him to walk under God's statutes and
keep His judgments. The word "cause" in Ezekiel 36:27 signifies
a compelling force coming from God's Holy Spirit into the man's
recreated spirit, helping him to know and keep God's judgments,
that is, to live and work for God.

When we receive Christ, we receive our new spirit and our new
heart. Our spirit is born again. Nothing changes about our flesh.
A newly saved Christian may look the same as he did before, but
the new creation—his new spirit—lives inside him. What he really
needs after the new birth is the Holy Spirit to help him with his
Christian life and service.

We should examine other Scriptures to gain a better
understanding of this matter. In Matthew's gospel, John the
Baptist declared that Jesus was the One who baptized with the
Holy Spirit.

> I indeed baptize you with water unto repentance, but
> He who is coming after me is mightier than I, whose
> sandals I am not worthy to carry. He will baptize you
> with the Holy Spirit and fire.
>
> —Matthew 3:11

John the Baptist could baptize anyone who desired to be a part of God's family, but John was incapable of baptizing anyone with the Holy Spirit. Jesus is the One who baptizes with the Holy Spirit. These are two different events. The pastor baptizes you with water after you are saved, that is, after you receive Christ as Lord and Savior. You are baptized with water after salvation just as Jesus was baptized by John to fulfill all righteousness. Many people believed in Jesus during His earthly ministry, but He never baptized a single person. His disciples performed the water baptisms (John 4:1, 2). This was a deliberate act on the part of our Savior. Jesus the Messiah and Savior of the world did not baptize men in water. A minister of the gospel baptizes with water anyone who believes in Jesus. In his gospel, John made sure everyone knew that Jesus did not baptize anyone with water. His baptism was with the Holy Spirit, not with water. He baptized with the Holy Spirit and with fire (Matthew 3:11).

Is it possible to be baptized in water and have no evidence of it? Is it possible to be baptized in water and not be wet right after baptism? The answer is no. When you are baptized in water, you are sure of what happened to you. You have the wet evidence. When Jesus baptizes with the Holy Spirit, you also come out of the experience wet. The wet evidence is speaking in tongues! Baptism in water is an event that involves a pastor, a candidate for baptism, a given time, and a set date. In most cases, others witness the event. Speaking in supernatural tongues can be heard by all and leaves no room for doubt or debate. If a man claims to have received Jesus' baptism, how else does he prove it to the world? On the day of Pentecost, the supernatural evidence the disciples had after their baptism by Jesus was the ability to speak in supernatural tongues.

Believers everywhere should go to Jesus Christ to receive His baptism instead of debating whether or not one can receive the Holy Spirit with or without the supernatural evidence of speaking in tongues. Speaking in tongues does not make one Christian better than another, but in the one who can, there is a greater potential for growth in the knowledge of God.

Saved, but not yet filled with the Holy Spirit

In chapter 8 of the book of Acts, Philip the evangelist was in Samaria preaching the gospel. Signs and wonders were performed in the name of the Lord Jesus Christ, and many received the Word of God. News of their conversion reached the apostles in Jerusalem, who sent Peter and John to the new believers in Samaria with a specific assignment: to help the new believers receive the Holy Spirit.

> Now when the apostles who were at Jerusalem heard that Samaria had received the word of God, they sent Peter and John to them, who, when they had come down, prayed for them that they might receive the Holy Spirit. (For as yet He was fallen upon none of them. They had only been baptized in the name of the Lord Jesus.) Then they laid hands on them, and they received the Holy Spirit.

—Acts 8:14-17

The above passage suggests that these new believers in Samaria had received Christ, but had not received the Holy Spirit. Is it possible to receive Christ and be saved without receiving the Holy Spirit? Many people believe that they were filled with the Holy Spirit on the day they were born again, but if that is the case, why was it so different for these Samaritan Christians? They received the message of the gospel, which means they had accepted Christ as Savior. They were baptized by Phillip, but they still needed to be filled with the Holy Spirit, according to the passage above. They needed prayer and hands laid upon them by the apostles Peter and John in order to receive the Holy Spirit.

The apostles understood fully their master's commandment, and went to carry out His will. When they arrived, they wasted no time and proceeded to lay their hands on the converts that they might receive the Holy Spirit. These events as written in the Word of God clearly show that receiving Christ to be born again and receiving the Holy Spirit for Christian living and service to God are two different events.

This is God's pattern for everyone who comes to Christ in humility. I am not sure why modern-day Christians believe that their experience with God should be different from that of the Samaritan believers. God has not changed, and this is the way of the Lord. You are saved, and then you are filled with the Holy Ghost, and can pray in tongues. The gift is given to those who thirst for more. If a believer is satisfied with how deep his faith in God is, he may cease in his pursuit of God. But let him remember that "deep calls unto deep," and "blessed are those who hunger and thirst for righteousness, for they shall be filled" (Psalm 42:7; Matthew 5:6). To obtain anything that will last on earth demands that we go deeper.

In chapter 19 of the book of Acts, Paul arrived at Ephesus and found twelve believers. He asked them if they had received the

Holy Spirit when they believed (Acts 19:2). Again, Paul's question suggests that one can believe and receive Christ without being filled with the Holy Spirit. The believers' answer was that they had not so much as heard whether there was a Holy Spirit (Acts 19:2). Then Paul asked, "Into what then were you baptized?" If they had been baptized into Jesus, they should have heard the word "Holy Spirit." Jesus had commanded that all believers be baptized in the name of the Father, the Son, and the Holy Spirit (Matthew 28:19). Their answer to Paul's second question was, "into John's baptism." That is they were baptized according the instruction given by John the Baptist. Paul instructed them on the new way to be baptized explaining to them that John's baptism was a baptism of repentance, but the new way was baptism into Christ.

Paul baptized them again in water, and then laid hands upon them for the Holy Spirit's baptism. I am sure he laid hands on them when he baptized them in water, but after the water baptism, he laid his hands on them again, but with another purpose in mind—the baptism of the Holy Spirit. The twelve were filled with the Holy Spirit after Paul laid hands on them, and all twelve of them spoke in tongues. Amazing!

Without a doubt, the salvation experience is separate from the Holy Spirit baptism. Every sincere believer should humble himself before the Word of God and honor God by praying to receive the baptism of the Holy Spirit. Just saying, "It is not so" will not change anything. Ask and you will receive, seek and you will find, knock and the door will be opened (Matthew 7:7). Just declaring that you do not accept something without researching it for yourself is a clear indication that you cannot be bothered. However, if you desire to have more of God, read on. I believe that God placed this book in your hands because He has seen that you want more of Him.

CHAPTER 7

DO ALL WHO RECEIVE THE HOLY SPIRIT SPEAK IN TONGUES?

Some Christians believe in the baptism of the Holy Spirit, but do not believe that all who receive the Holy Spirit speak in tongues. They believe that there are other gifts that are also a sign one has received the Holy Spirit. The problem with this position is that there is hardly any Scriptural support for it. Also, most people who take this position cannot point to anything supernatural in nature taking place in their own lives.

On the day of Pentecost, 120 disciples waited for the promise of the Father. The Holy Spirit appeared to them as cloven tongues of fire. The disciples were all filled with the Holy Spirit and began to speak in tongues as the Spirit gave them utterance (Acts 2:1-4). If it were God's design for some believers to speak in tongues, but for others to manifest other gifts, He would have demonstrated this on the day of Pentecost. God had 120 people to do so with what He pleased. The fact that every one of them spoke in tongues on the very first day the

Holy Spirit came is a clear indication that God wants all believers to receive the Holy Spirit and speak with tongues. Personally, it would have been unacceptable to me if I had been among them on the day of Pentecost but could not speak in tongues like the others.

In chapter 10 of the book of Acts, Cornelius the Centurion called together all of his close friends and relatives to hear the gospel from the mouth of the apostle Peter. As Peter presented the gospel, the Holy Spirit fell on all within the house, and the Jews who had come with Peter knew that God had filled all the Gentiles in Cornelius' home with the Holy Spirit on that glorious day. How did they know? They heard them speaking in tongues. The Bible does not tell us how many were in Cornelius' home, but we do know that they all spoke in tongues.

The Bible says nothing about "tongues of fire" in this instance. There was no record of "a rushing mighty wind." Hearing the Gentiles speak in tongues was the only way the Jews with Peter could tell that they had also received the Holy Spirit. I believe this was God's message that this was the way to tell when a person had received the Holy Spirit (Acts 10:44-46). All of the Jews who received the Holy Spirit on the day of Pentecost spoke in tongues, and all of the Gentiles who received the Holy Spirit in Cornelius' home spoke in tongues. Therefore, all who receive the Holy Spirit will speak in tongues; the gospel went to the Jews first, and then the Gentiles. God was showing us that He treats everyone who comes to receive in the same manner. All of His children will be able to speak with tongues when they receive the Holy Spirit. This is the Lord's doing, and it is marvelous in our sight.

Those who claim that the gift of tongues was given on the day of Pentecost so that those who gathered in Jerusalem for the feast could hear the gospel in their own language cannot lay hold of any preaching to that effect in Cornelius' home. Peter did the only preaching on that day, and he did not do it in tongues. Tongues came after the preaching. This should prove that the gift of tongues was not given by God to be used for preaching; rather, it is primarily our prayer language.

The Bible tells us that in the mouth of two or three witnesses every word may be established (2 Corinthians 13:1). Here we have two instances (Acts 2:1-4 and Acts 10:44-46) in which everyone who was filled with the Holy Spirit spoke in tongues. A third instance is recorded in chapter 19 of Acts. Paul laid his hands on twelve men after baptizing them in water to receive the Holy Spirit. All twelve disciples received the Holy Spirit after Paul prayed for them, and all spoke in tongues.

No one should feel like less of a Christian because he or she does not speak in tongues, but if you want to be filled with all of God, when that is done, you will be filled with more of the Holy Spirit. The Holy Spirit is God; God is a spirit.

In 1 Corinthians, Paul said, "I thank my God I speak with tongues more than you all, yet in the church I would rather speak five words with my understanding, that I may teach others also, than ten thousand words in a tongue" (1 Corinthians 14:18-19). His statement suggests that everyone at the church at Corinth could speak in tongues, but Paul spent more time than others doing so in private. I wonder how Paul found enough time to do this, and why? Speaking in tongues must have been very important to Paul as a Christian if he spent so much time doing it. What benefit did he think he would derive? Why do Christians today not do the same? Could it be that the enemy has deceived us into ignoring a very potent weapon against him? Could this be why Christians today seem so powerless and confused about faith?

When Paul was filled with the Holy Spirit (Acts 9:17), nothing was said about whether or not he spoke in tongues. A skeptic

may point to this and conclude that the gift of tongues is not a sign or the initial evidence of being filled with the Holy Spirit. However, Paul often spoke in tongues in prayer to God. Similarly, nothing is said about the new Samaritan believers receiving the Holy Spirit and speaking in tongues when Peter and John laid hands on them to receive the Holy Spirit. However, it is clear that something supernatural took place and got the attention of Simon the sorcerer (Acts 8:18-24). He was willing to give money to gain the same power that was at work in Peter and John. I believe that he saw the people who had received the Holy Spirit speaking in other tongues as hands were laid on them. No other Biblical signs are consistently associated with receiving the Holy Spirit.

Receiving the Holy Spirit is a great part of the blessing of Abraham

I believe God left us with no doubt that He wants all of His children to be filled with the Holy Spirit and to receive the pure language from heaven, our prayer language. We should not be afraid of the gift that God offers freely through the redemptive work of Christ. Christ has redeemed us from the curse of the law, "Cursed is everyone who hangs on a tree," that the blessing of Abraham might come upon the Gentiles, that we might receive the promise of the Spirit through faith (Galatians 3:13-14). Part of our redemption from the curse of the law is being able to receive the promise of the Father, the Holy Spirit. The Holy Spirit is the One to guide us and usher us into the Blessing of Abraham. He teaches, He guides, He comforts, and He helps us with our prayer life. Receive the Holy Spirit in Jesus' name today. Amen!

These signs follow those who believe

Obviously, not all believers speak in tongues, but if we examine closely what Jesus said in Mark chapter 16, I believe we can conclude that God wants all of His children to be able to speak in tongues. Jesus spoke of the signs that should follow all believers. The believers do not follow the signs; rather, the signs follow the believers. Anyone can claim to be a follower of Christ, but Jesus said that some signs follow true followers.

> He who believes and is baptized will be saved; but he who does not believe will be condemned. And these signs will follow those who believe: In My name they will cast out demons; they will speak with new tongues. They will take up serpents; and if they drink anything deadly, it will by no means hurt them; they will lay hands on the sick, and they will recover.
>
> —Mark 16:17-18

Those who argue that not all believers can speak in tongues believe that everyone is given a gift, and that there are other gifts than that of tongues. The flaws in this reasoning are apparent when you meditate on the passage above. Is it true that only some disciples can cast out devils? Is it God's plan for some of His children to be powerless against devils? Is it true that some may drink deadly things and remain unhurt, while others dare not because they have a different gift? Who are the people with the gift of drinking deadly poisons? Can only some gifted believers pray and lay hands on the sick to heal them? Is that what God intended for the church? If the person with the gift of healing is out of town and a man comes to church to find healing from God, then the man must wait for

LANGUAGE FROM HEAVEN

the "healer" to return to town. Is this the way God works? Would God really have his gift of healing tied to one special person? In reality, no man is the gift of healing; neither is any man the gift of tongues. The Holy Spirit has the gifts, and the glory is to God, not to man. Everyone who is willing can be used. Everyone who is a believer and is willing can speak in tongues.

One Sunday morning, in the city where I grew up in Nigeria, I was preparing to go to church and I was running late. One of my family members called out to me that a couple of Jehovah's witnesses wanted to talk to me about God. I thought to myself, "These men will surely hold me up and I will be late for church service." I prayed silently for God to help me not to be rude to them, but be able to leave them with a gospel message that might make them think about their faith in a new light. I wanted my encounter with them to be brief and to the point so that I would be able to get to church on time. So I went out to meet them while still talking to God in my heart. Immediately, I had an idea! I greeted them and asked them what their mission was. They said they wanted to talk to me about becoming a Christian. I replied, "How can you talk to me about becoming a Christian when you are not one?"

They were shocked and speechless. Before they had a chance to recover, I quickly offered to prove my point using the Bible they were carrying with them. I turned to Mark 16:17-18 and read, "And these signs will follow those who believe: In My name they will cast out demons; they will speak with new tongues. They will take up serpents; and if they drink anything deadly, it will by no means hurt them; they will lay hands on the sick, and they will recover." I asked them if they thought that Jesus was telling us how to identify a true Christian? They could not deny that that was the implication and agreed with me. I asked them if they had ever cast out a devil in their Christian experiences. They answered, "No." I replied, "Well, I told you that you are not true Christians." I went down the list. They seemed horrified about the idea of speaking in tongues. I told them that they were deceived and that they needed to find out more about the Savior and how to be saved. They left confused. I prayed that God would help them come to the true knowledge of our Lord Jesus Christ.

I know there are many born-again Christians who have not experienced these signs in their lives. The reason is that they have not been taught about the gifts or the baptism of the Holy Spirit. What bothers me most is that people don't seem to care enough to carefully investigate speaking in tongues and the baptism of the Holy Spirit. Are they afraid of the supernatural, of things we are unfamiliar with? Why would any child of God be afraid to discover a truth that the Bible teaches? Some allow themselves to be led by others in the faith who oppose speaking in tongues, but these individuals may have had doubts and misunderstandings about the Holy Spirit's baptism, and possibly about other matters of faith. Should a man build his life on the opinions of others rather than on the Word of God? It doesn't matter who these others claim to be or how highly esteemed they are. Would God ignore His own Word to honor the opinions of supposedly great men?

Some people have concluded that speaking in tongues is not a tool for today's church because they previously tried to receive it, but nothing happened. Do not try to receive; just receive! Jesus did not ask us to try to receive, but to receive. I believe this book can help those who truly want to receive by aiding them in their search for answers in the Scriptures. Faith comes through understanding what is written in the Word. What you comprehend in the Word of God brings you deliverance. Comprehension may be through a Bible reading, a message in a book, or a message by sign language.

Faith comes through comprehension, and brings with it deliverance. Faith to receive the Holy Spirit can be by reading the Bible itself or a book like this one that tells what the Bible has to say on the subject. Once you gain understanding, you are on your way to true freedom.

Praying in the spirit

Another reason I believe that it is God's will for believers to pray in tongues is that God tells us to pray in the Spirit: "But you, beloved, building yourselves up on your most holy faith, praying in the Holy Spirit" (Jude 1:20). Paul tells us, "For if I pray in a tongue, my spirit prays, but my understanding is unfruitful. What is the conclusion then? I will pray with the spirit, and I will also pray with the understanding. I will sing with the spirit, and I will also sing with the understanding" (1 Corinthians 14:14-15).

This Scripture suggests that praying in tongues is the same thing as praying in the spirit. You cannot pray in the Spirit without praying in tongues. Secondly, if you can understand what you are saying in prayer, then you are not praying in the Spirit. There is nothing wrong with praying in a language you understand, but if you are doing so, you are not praying in the Spirit.

In the book of Jude, God told us to pray in the Spirit, which means to pray in tongues. Why would God command this when, according to some, not all Christians have the gift of tongues? The fact that God instructs us this way suggests that it is His will for all Christians to be able to speak in tongues. If the gift of tongues were not available to all, it would be wrong for God to tell all believers to pray in the Holy Spirit knowing only some could do so. That would put those who could not speak in tongues at a disadvantage, in a different class of believers. Surely, this is not God's design or desire. Let us be careful not to confuse our unbelief with doctrine by telling those hungry for more of God that the gift of tongues is not a tool for us today.

Paul instructed us to put on the whole armor of God as we wrestle "against principalities, against powers, against the rulers of the darkness of this age, against spiritual hosts of wickedness in the heavenly places" (Ephesians 6:12). Then he told us, "Pray always with all prayer and supplication in the Spirit, being watchful to this end with all perseverance and supplication for all the saints" (Ephesians 6:18). Praying in the Spirit is different from praying an inspired prayer. When we are inspired in prayer, our words come from our own spirit, in our own natural language. But praying in the Spirit is praying in tongues. "For he who speaks in a tongue does not speak to men but to God, for no one understands him; however, in the Spirit he speaks mysteries" (1 Corinthians 14:2).

One who speaks in tongues does not himself understand what he is saying, and neither can anyone else. God keeps the mystery to Himself. But the prayer releases the blessings of heaven onto the believer, despite his lack of understanding. He who speaks in tongues speaks directly to God in a supernatural language.

CHAPTER 8

THE BENEFITS OF SPEAKING IN TONGUES

Some have asked why praying in tongues is necessary when God can understand us when we pray in our natural language. We often lean on our own understanding and do not trust in the Lord with all our hearts. His Word has all the answers we need for life and godliness. While we may never fully understand why God chose this way for us to effectively communicate with Him, we are blessed if we are willing and obedient (Isaiah 1:19). The Bible tells us that "the secret things belong to the Lord our God, but those things which are revealed belong to us, and our children forever" (Deuteronomy 29:29).

What we do know is that the baptism of the Holy Spirit produces the ability to speak in tongues. When we speak in tongues, the Holy Spirit is at work, helping our spirits to communicate with God. Paul told us that when we speak in tongues, our spirit prays, but our understanding is unfruitful (1 Corinthians 14:14). The word "spirit" in this passage is not capitalized, so Paul was talking about the born-again human spirit. We must do the praying, but the Holy Spirit is the one who supernaturally gives voice to our human spirits by way of the tongues of men and of angels (1 Corinthians 13:1). That is what happened on the day of Pentecost when the disciples were filled with the Holy Spirit. They did the speaking, but the Holy Ghost gave the utterance (Acts 2:4).

The Holy Spirit will not give utterance if the believer refuses to do the speaking. He is responsible for the language that comes out, but first, the believer must speak. When one willingly gives over the most powerful part of his body, the tongue, to the Holy Spirit, things change for the better in his life. The benefits of speaking in tongues can clearly be seen in the Scriptures if one reads with an open mind.

The lives of the disciples

The lives of the disciples are one obvious example that speaking in tongues provides great benefit to the Christian life. Jesus had a hard time getting His disciples to understand the kingdom of God. The disciples had arguments amongst themselves. They were also very fearful and often confused about what Jesus was saying. Peter denied Jesus to a servant girl. The disciples fled and hid themselves after Jesus' arrest. They were afraid of those in power and stayed in hiding until long after Jesus rose from the dead. They seemed clueless about the mission Christ had given to them, even after He rose from the dead. However, after the day of Pentecost, the disciples were a different bunch! They became fearless and full of understanding and confidence, and they openly confessed their faith in Jesus.

Peter and John told the leaders who put Jesus to death that they would rather obey God than man. They knew they might be killed, but that did not matter to them.

So they called them and commanded them not to speak at all nor teach in the name of Jesus. But Peter and John answered and said to them, "Whether it is right in the sight of God to listen to you more than to God, you judge. For we cannot but speak the things which we have seen and heard."

—Acts 4:18-20

They were changed! Their misunderstanding or confusion about the mission Jesus gave them was gone. What made the difference? What happened to change these fearful believers into bold and fearless individuals in a matter of days? It was the coming of the Holy Spirit from heaven on the day of Pentecost to take over the work Jesus began. They received the Holy Spirit on that day and man spoke in tongues for the first time. That divine event changed the disciples' lives! The church was born on that day.

The Lord has not changed, and His church also remains the same because of Him. The speaking in tongues on that day was not done in secret; men from all over the world heard the disciples speak in tongues that day and were amazed. Peter explained that they were witnessing the fulfillment of the prophecy of Joel in the Old Testament:

But this is what was spoken by the prophet Joel: "And it shall come to pass in the last days, says God, that I will pour out of My Spirit on all flesh."

—Acts 2:16-17

We are still living in the last days. God still pours out His Spirit upon all flesh. All who received the Holy Spirit on the day of Pentecost spoke in tongues. All who receive the Holy Spirit today will speak in tongues in fulfillment of the prophecy of Joel. Otherwise, the prophecy of Joel has been only partially fulfilled.

Jesus had instructed the disciples to wait in Jerusalem for the promise of the Father. Jesus said, "But you shall receive power when the Holy Spirit has come upon you; and you shall be witnesses to Me in Jerusalem, and in all Judea and Samaria, and to the end of the earth" (Acts 1:8). They needed the power of the Holy Spirit to make them fearless. They were to be witnesses of the resurrection of the Savior before a skeptical world. They would be opposed, lied about, threatened, and murdered, but none of these things would move them, because they received power from the Holy Spirit. This is the only way their witness would have been possible.

In chapter 4 of Acts, the disciples prayed for boldness so that they could do what God had called them to do. The same people who killed Jesus had threatened them and told them to stop preaching the gospel in their city. They prayed to God to make them fearless and bold in preaching the message of Jesus Christ. God answered, and the Bible tells us that the place where they prayed was shaken, and they were filled with the Holy Spirit and preached the Word of God with boldness (Acts 4:28-31).

The Spirit helps our weaknesses

One of the great blessings of praying in the language from heaven is that our minds need not know the true nature of the problem. We saw in Chapter 5 of this book that we do not know what to pray for, but we ought to be specific in our requests when we pray to God. The Holy Spirit helps us with this weakness.

Jesus told us that the spirit is willing, but the flesh is weak (Matthew 26:41). Our spirits are always ready to pray, fight, and

be victorious, but our flesh is weak. The power of the Holy Spirit coupled with our willingness can help us overcome the weaknesses of the flesh. In 1976, a year after I gave my life to Christ, I was greatly persecuted because of my faith. I heard people in the little town where I lived saying that I had lost my mind and become a mad man. I ignored it because I knew I was sane. I considered this talk to be lies of the Devil to prevent other young men and women from receiving Christ. But the gossip bothered my loving mother and she decided to do something about it.

I was renting a home in order to get away from family members who did not understand what had happened to me and were resentful of my new faith. From there, I was taken by force to a village deep in the jungle of Nigeria to see a witch doctor who had been highly recommended to my mother. I will not go into the details of my experience in this book, but suffice it to say that I ended up with my hands chained together at the wrist and one leg chained to a wall. I lay on the floor of that little room feeling sorry for myself, wondering how becoming a Christian could have placed me in this situation. I was confused. I cried and prayed, but I did not know what to say to God. I was uncomfortable because I could not use my hands to pillow my head because of the chains.

I badly needed rest because of the events of that day and the day before. All I could do was pray in tongues, asking God for mercy. Before long, late that night, God answered. A voice spoke to me. I thought at first that I was just hearing my own thoughts, but now I know that the Lord was speaking to me. He said, "The chains are loose. Why don't you take your hands out of them?" I checked the chains, and indeed they were loose. I was amazed! I played with them a little and freed my hands. I was grateful to God and had a good night's rest. I was exhausted.

Very early the next morning, while it was still dark, two men who worked with the witch doctor came into the room. They were sure my hands were still chained. I sat up as they chanted and tried to cast their spell on me in that dark room with only a little lamp for light. They had a giant bell with them, and they rang the bell as they chanted. I paid them no attention, but the loud sound of the bell in that little room was painful to hear. I asked them if their spell would not work if they stopped ringing the bell. I complained that the sound was hurting my ears, but they went on with their act without saying a word to me.

Suddenly, the voice that had spoken to me during the night spoke again. He reminded me that my hands were free, and asked me to take the bell from them and force them to chant without their bell. As soon as I reached out with my hand to take the bell, fear came over them. They did not expect my hands to be free. They ran out of the room with haste and disappeared into the darkness. Without thinking, I ran after them. Only when I was standing outside the door did I realize that I was totally free of their chains. I did not have even one link of the chain on me. The witch doctor was quick to release me from his compound that morning. He refunded the full amount of money he had received to work his enchantment on me. "Take this boy out of my yard," he said to my mother. He wanted nothing to do with me.

I give God the glory for my deliverance on that fateful day and I thank God for giving us the ability to pray in tongues. When we do not know what to pray for, the Holy Spirit Himself intercedes for us in accordance with the will of God.

My mother, who later gave her life to Christ, could not stop laughing as we left the witch doctor's compound. She asked me to ask the Lord to forgive her, because she had acted in ignorance. She said everyone around her believed that I had lost my mind, and she had felt she had to do something to help her son. I told her God had forgiven her, and then asked why she was laughing so much. She replied, "I am laughing at the way those men took off into the darkness!" She never asked me how I got free. I think she believed God had done it.

Strength for our faith

Another benefit of praying in tongues is that it strengthens our faith in God. The Bible has a lot to say about the importance of faith. The word of God tells us that by grace, we are saved through faith (Ephesians 2:8). The just shall live by faith (Romans 1:17). We walk by faith and not by sight (2 Corinthians 5:7). Our Christian walk is a walk of faith. Our fight is the good fight of faith (1 Timothy 6:12). The victory that overcomes the world is our faith (1 John 5:4).

The importance of faith in our Christian life cannot be overemphasized. It is of vital importance. No wonder God gave us the ability to pray in tongues as the Spirit gives utterance to strengthen our faith in Him. The Bible says, "But you, beloved, building yourselves up on your most holy faith, praying in the Holy Spirit" (Jude 1:20).

The Bible tells us to be strong in the Lord and in the power of His might, and to put on the whole armor of God so we can withstand the wiles of the Devil (Ephesians 6:10-11). Strength in the Lord is a requirement for us to stand up against the tricks of the Devil. We will not be able to recognize the wiles of the Devil if we are not strong in the Lord. Strength in the Lord has nothing to do with our physical strength; it has everything to do with our spiritual muscles. If faith is the victory that overcomes the world, then faith is the muscle we need to overcome the Devil. To be strong in the Lord is to be strong in faith, and praying in tongues will strengthen our faith (Jude 1:20).

Paul said in 1 Corinthians 14:4 that he who speaks in a tongue edifies himself. To edify means to enlighten, inform, educate, instruct, improve, or teach. If faith comes from hearing the Word of God, then praying in tongues is receiving supernatural instruction. When we pray in tongues, we do not speak to other men; no one understands what we are saying in tongues. The Bible tells us that we speak mysteries (1 Corinthians 14:2). The mysteries we speak in tongues supernaturally enlighten our born-again spirits; they educate, instruct, teach, and edify us supernaturally (1 Corinthians 14:4). This builds up our faith. We may not understand exactly how speaking in tongues builds our faith, but we must trust that the Author of our faith knows what He is talking about. If we are willing and obedient, we shall eat the good of the land (Isaiah 1:19). We do not have to understand how it works; all we have to do is to be obedient.

Enter His rest

Many Christians have been saved for a long time, but they are still struggling in the turmoil of life. They have not found rest in God. There seems to be no real peace for them. Some of these individuals have been baptized in the Holy Spirit, but long ago stopped speaking in tongues. Some of them have allowed Satan to place doubt in their hearts about the gift they received from God. This is a trick of the Devil's to keep them bound.

Jesus said, "Come to Me, all you who labor and are heavy laden, and I will give you rest" (Matthew 11:28). If you have come to

Jesus but still do not have rest, you may want to seek Him for the baptism of the Holy Spirit. But remember, you must use the gift often in your prayer life if you truly want to enter into His rest.

> For with stammering lips and another tongue He will speak to this people, to whom He said, "This is the rest with which you may cause the weary to rest," And, "This is the refreshing"; yet they would not hear.
> —Isaiah 28:11-12

"Stammering lips" means speaking in tongues (1 Corinthians 14:21). This is how to find rest for your soul. If your spirit needs refreshing, spend time praying in tongues. Sometimes, ten minutes of prayer are enough; other times, one hour is not enough. Do whatever it takes to enter into His rest. Praying often in tongues will usher you into the Master's rest. Pay no attention to thoughts that may go through your mind saying you are not accomplishing much. Stay with it, and true rest will be delivered to you.

Revelation from God

The Bible tells us that secrets belong to the Lord our God, but things that are revealed belong to us and to our children (Deuteronomy 29:29). This means that what God chooses to keep secret will not benefit us here on earth. Yet there are mysteries in the Word that He wants revealed for our benefit. The Bible tells us that our children will benefit from the revelations we receive from the Lord.

Jesus said to His disciples, "It has been given to you to know the mysteries of the kingdom of heaven, but to them it has not been given" (Matthew 13:11). The kingdom of heaven is shrouded in mysteries, but we can know them through the power of the Holy Spirit—this is of great benefit to us in our present lives. But just because it is given to us to know the mysteries does not mean we do not have to do all we can to unlock them. I believe the more of the mysteries of the kingdom of God you are able to unlock, the more powerful a Christian you will be in this life.

The Bible stated that God's people are destroyed because of their lack of knowledge (Hosea 4:6). Many have the knowledge of the Word, but they lack understanding. Jesus told us that if one has heard the Word of God but does not understand it, the wicked one immediately comes to steal the Word from his heart (Matthew 13:19). Understanding is the key to victory. Faith comes through revelation. That is why Paul never ceased to pray for God to give the Christians in Ephesus the spirit of wisdom and revelation in the knowledge of Him. Paul wanted them to be enlightened so they could know the hope of their calling (Ephesians 1:16-18). Knowing or receiving revelation is vital to our Christian walk. What you do not understand in God's word, you cannot enjoy. It is knowledge of truth that makes us free (John 8:32).

One of the best ways to receive revelation is to spend time praying in tongues. When we pray in tongues, the Holy Spirit assists our spirits to pray. This is very much a supernatural event. Our spirits can never be closer to the Spirit of God than they are when we pray in tongues. I believe that in such closeness, the Spirit can easily pass secrets from God on to our own human spirits. Consider the following scripture:

> But as it is written: "Eye has not seen, nor ear heard, nor have entered into the heart of man the things which God has prepared for those who love Him." But

God has revealed them to us through His Spirit. For the Spirit searches all things, yes, the deep things of God. For what man knows the things of a man except the spirit of the man which is in him? Even so no one knows the things of God except the Spirit of God. Now we have received, not the spirit of the world, but the Spirit who is from God, that we might know the things that have been freely given to us by God.

—1 Corinthians 2:9-12

The things that the eye has not seen, that the ear has not heard, and that have not entered the hearts of men are things for us to enjoy here on earth. They are privileges for us, as children of God—but we have to know of them first. The Bible contains God's will for our lives. We must read and understand His will as written. We cannot benefit from it unless we know and understand what is in it for us. The Holy Spirit was given to help us know and understand God's will, and so that the Devil would not beat us out of our inheritance by lying to us about God's will.

How do we get the Holy Spirit to help us understand God's will? As we seek God by praying in tongues, the Holy Spirit makes secret things known to us. Paul said, "we have received . . . the Spirit who is from God, that we might know the things that have been freely given to us by God" (1 Corinthians 2:12). Just because we have received the Spirit does not mean He will automatically reveal these things to us. We need to spend time fellowshipping with the Holy Spirit, and there is no better way to do this than to pray in the Spirit. We must ask to receive, we must seek to find, and we must knock for the door to be opened for us (Matthew 7:7). Men who have found the secret of praying in tongues have risen to become great soldiers of the cross.

THE APOSTLE PAUL OFTEN SPOKE IN TONGUES

Paul is considered the greatest of the apostles. He wrote more than half of the New Testament books. Paul suffered more than any of the other disciples for his faith in Christ. He pursued God as no other man has since the beginning of the world, and he received the greatest revelation of all. Paul was not an apostle who walked with Jesus in the flesh, yet he had a greater understanding of the Christian message than all those who ate and walked with Jesus, heard His teachings, and witnessed His miracles as they traveled from place to place preaching the Word.

In Galatians, Paul wrote, "But I make known to you, brethren, that the gospel which was preached by me is not according to man. For I neither received it from man, nor was I taught it, but it came through the revelation of Jesus Christ" (Galatians 1:11-12). If Paul was not taught the message that he preached, then God must have given it to him without human help, by revelation.

 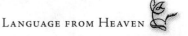

Paul was filled with the Holy Spirit when Ananias laid his hand on him after encountering the Lord Jesus on the road to Damascus (Acts 9:17). We are not told Paul spoke in tongues then. However, in his instruction to the Corinthian church on the use of the gifts of the Holy Spirit, he proclaimed that he spoke in tongues more than any one of them. "I thank my God I speak with tongues more than you all, yet in the church I would rather speak five words with my understanding, that I may teach others also, than ten thousand words in a tongue" (1 Corinthians 14:18-19).

If Paul did not speak in tongues in church, then where was he doing it, and for what purpose? This was one of the ways Paul practiced his faith and devotion to God. The question is, why was he so confident that he spoke in tongues more than everyone else? The people in the church at Corinth were very zealous for spiritual gifts (1 Corinthians 14:12). How did Paul know without hesitation that he spoke in tongues more than they? Paul spent much time praying to God in tongues outside the church, in private, for his own edification. If Paul could say by the inspiration of the Holy Spirit that he spoke in tongues more often than anyone else, then I believe no human being who has lived on this side of the cross of Jesus Christ spent more time praying in tongues than the apostle Paul. Paul believed that praying in tongues was an integral part of his Christian life, and that doing so made him a better Christian. It would be hard to explain otherwise why he did pray in tongues so much. He had a great deal of responsibility as a minister of the gospel. He was responsible for the salvation of Gentile Christians, but he still set aside much time to pray in tongues to God.

Why was the one man who spoke in tongues more than everyone else the one who received the greatest revelation about our Lord Jesus Christ? Paul was a disciple, just like the rest of us, but the revelation he received from God regarding the gospel is still changing lives today. I believe Paul's devotion to the gospel of our Lord Jesus Christ, coupled with his prayer language, resulted in his great success in Christianity. He was certainly an amazing man. However, all credit goes to the power of the Holy Spirit in his life, and the sacrifice of our Lord Jesus Christ.

Paul's devotion underscores the importance of praying in tongues. Paul said, "Imitate me, just as I also imitate Christ" (1 Corinthians 11:1). If we must follow the faith of our fathers, then we must follow and imitate Paul, who was a true follower of Christ and apostle to the Gentiles. By God's providence, today Paul is an apostle not only to the gentiles, but to all who believe in the Lord Jesus Christ as Savior. His writings are still a source of wisdom and comfort to everyone who wants to know God more.

How did Paul receive the message of the gospel he preached if men did not teach him? Paul was educated in the school of Gamaliel (Acts 22:3). He knew the Scriptures, but did not know or understand the gospel message before he was converted. After Jesus rose from the dead, He did not pull out a chair to sit down and teach Paul one-on-one the message of the gospel. Paul got it from the teachings of the Holy Spirit. This was the revelation that came to Him.

> For what man knows the things of a man except the spirit of the man which is in him? Even so no one knows the things of God except the Spirit of God. Now we have received, not the spirit of the world, but the Spirit who is from God, that we might know the things that have been freely given to us by God.
>
> —1 Corinthians 2:11-12

In essence, Paul revealed how he got the revelation from God: through the Holy Spirit. The Holy Spirit is the Spirit of truth. He

 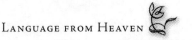

is the only One who knows the deep secrets of God and can search them out for the purpose of revealing them to man. However, a man must be willing to engage the Holy Spirit as his teacher. He must spend much time gaining knowledge and understanding from the Holy Spirit. Jesus said the Holy Spirit is a teacher (John 14:26). Paul engaged the Holy Spirit by spending much time praying in tongues.

To engage the Holy Spirit, we must spend time with Him, and there is no better way to do so than in prayer, especially with the supernatural language of the Holy Spirit. You cannot receive instruction in a language that you do not speak or understand. However, you can speak supernaturally in a language you do not understand and still receive edification from the Holy Spirit. The Holy Spirit transmits the deep truths of God into your spirit, and your eyes open to the truth. Once this happens, no one can keep you down. No one can keep you bound. The Devil and all the hosts of hell cannot keep you in bondage. Freedom comes with the revelation of truth from the Holy Spirit. Jesus said, "You shall know the truth, and the truth shall make you free" (John 8:32). Freedom comes through the knowledge of the truths of the gospel of Jesus Christ. Here, "knowledge" means spiritual understanding or revelation. Many people know what the Scriptures say, but they do not have real understanding of them, so they are not able to truly position themselves to receive God's deliverance.

> And in them the prophecy of Isaiah is fulfilled, which says: "Hearing you will hear and shall not understand, and seeing you will see and not perceive; for the hearts of this people have grown dull. Their ears are hard of hearing, and their eyes they have closed, lest they should see with their eyes and hear with their ears, lest

they should understand with their hearts and turn, So
that I should heal them."

—Matthew 13:14-15

Once a person receives revelation, he is freed from bondage. This freedom is the wisdom, from God, to be able to separate oneself from whatever is causing one problems in life. This is the way God wants it. Jesus came so that everyone alive in Him could have life more abundantly (John 10:10). This is God's will for everyone. God has no favorites; everyone is His favorite. If you seek, you will find (Matthew 7:7).

Paul spent much time edifying himself as he prayed in tongues and words of revelation were poured into his spirit. God has many precious things in store for us to enjoy in this life, but we cannot know them without the help of the Holy Spirit. It is the Holy Spirit given by God who helps us to know what has been freely given to us. Jesus said, "when He, the Spirit of truth, has come, He will guide you into all truth" (John 16:13). Jesus said, "the Holy Spirit . . . will teach you all things, and bring to remembrance all things that I said to you" (John 14:26). The Holy Spirit holds the key to God's revelations. Paul stayed close to the Holy Spirit by engaging his pure language from heaven, and he was taught by the Holy Spirit. The Holy Spirit gave Paul the spirit of wisdom and revelation in knowledge of Jesus Christ. Paul prayed to God for all believers to have this spirit of revelation (Ephesians 1:15-22). We can achieve this quickly if we pray in tongues more often.

Paul said that "he who speaks in a tongue does not speak to men but to God, for no one understands him; however, in the spirit he speaks mysteries" (1 Corinthians 14:2). If a man speaks mysteries to God, who understands all mystery, who benefits? Does God benefit from mysteries spoken by a man? Could a man teach God?

LANGUAGE FROM HEAVEN

I believe the speaking of mysteries during prayer in tongues is for the benefit of the one speaking. If a man keeps on speaking these mysteries from his spirit or heart as he prays in tongues to God, then before long, his spirit will begin to pick up on the mysteries he is speaking. This is revelation! The spirit of a believer is never closer to the Spirit of God than when he is praying in tongues. The Spirit of God helps give utterance to the spirit of man in tongues as the man prays. The Holy Spirit is actively engaged, and in a state like this, anything is possible. Supernatural transactions can occur between the Spirit of God and the spirit of man. This is a thing that God wants so that His will can be done on earth.

Paul said that although he speaks in tongues often, he would rather speak five words with his understanding during a church service so that he may teach others also than ten thousand words in tongues (1 Corinthians 14:18-19). Paul's statement implied that he received instruction when he prayed in tongues; the church was not the place to do that. In church, he used only his own language so he could teach others. He instructed himself in the Spirit when he prayed privately in tongues, but he instructed others in a known language in church. He drew from what he was informed about in prayer by the Holy Spirit to instruct believers in church so that they can grow in faith through the revelations he had received.

I believe praying in tongues is one key way the Holy Spirit teaches us. Paul knew it, so he spent so much time praying in tongues that he could say, "I thank my God I speak in tongues more than you all." Paul's revelations about the gospel came through the Holy Spirit's teaching. I believe that as Paul spent time fellowshipping with the Holy Spirit and praying in tongues, the Holy Spirit, our Teacher from heaven, deposited truths into his spirit. Paul said that the Holy Spirit reveals the secrets of God (1 Corinthians 2:10-12).

Stir up the gift of God inside you

One of the mistakes made by those who have received the Holy Spirit is to assume that because they have received the Holy Spirit, the works of the Spirit will automatically be evident in their lives. They yearn for the boldness that comes with the baptism of the Holy Spirit, but they find themselves slaves of fear and uncertain about many things concerning the kingdom of God. They lack the confidence in God that should accompany the baptism of the Holy Spirit. The problem is that every gift of God must be fanned into flames by the believer before the benefit of the gift is evident. Deep calls out to deep (Psalm 42:7). The gifts of the Spirit come with the Holy Spirit's baptism, and by the laying on of hands, but if the believer refuses to believe enough in the gifts within to stir them up, no one benefits.

Paul instructed Timothy, "Do not neglect the gift that is in you, which was given to you by prophecy with the laying on of the hands of the eldership" (1 Timothy 4:14). Gifts were given to Timothy by prophecy and by the elders' laying on of hands. Timothy was a young man. Like most people today, Timothy must have thought to himself, they believe I have these gifts because they laid hands on me and prophesied. I am not sure about all these things. However, Paul who knew much about stirring up a gift through its constant use, reminded him to not only believe in the gifts, but also not neglect them.

> Therefore I remind you to stir up the gift of God which is in you through the laying on of my hands. For God has not given us a spirit of fear, but of power and of love and of a sound mind.
>
> —2 Timothy 1:6-7

God will not stir up the gift that He has given you. It is your own responsibility to stir it up if you want to benefit from it. No one will benefit from the mighty gifts God has given them through the Holy Spirit if they refuse to use the gifts as needed. Paul knew the benefit of praying in tongues, and he did so more than any other man. Every believer who has received the baptism of the Holy Spirit and can pray in tongues has the responsibility of stirring up the gift by spending lots of time praying in other tongues so that he and the world can benefit from it.

Paul's great revelation in the gospel

Paul told us by revelation that salvation does not come from keeping the ten commandments but rather by grace through faith in our Lord Jesus Christ (Ephesians 2:8-9). In chapters 7 and 8 of the book of Romans, Paul revealed to us the nature of the fallen man, his struggle with sin, and the power of the gospel to deliver him. Paul told us repeatedly that the just shall live by faith (Romans 1:17; Galatians 3:11). This is a fundamental truth that is central in our walk with God. In chapter 13 of 1 Corinthians, Paul revealed to us the preeminence of love. Paul also revealed the different manifestations of the Holy Spirit during worship in chapter 12 of 1 Corinthians. The apostle Peter acknowledged that Paul had received great revelations from the Lord.

> And consider that the longsuffering of our Lord is
> salvation—as also our beloved brother Paul, according
> to the wisdom given to him, has written to you, as
> also in all his epistles, speaking in them of these
> things, in which are some things hard to understand,

which untaught and unstable people twist to their own destruction, as they do also the rest of the Scriptures.

—2 Peter 3:15-16

The one who spoke in tongues the most received the greatest insight into the truths of the gospel of our Lord and Savior Jesus Christ. The revelation God gave Paul can be unveiled to us if we do what Paul did, and often pray privately in tongues to God. It is hard to truly understand Scriptures without the help of the Holy Spirit. He has been given to us to help in every area of life, both our natural and spiritual lives. He is the Helper.

CHAPTER 10

RECEIVING THE HOLY SPIRIT

That great day of the feast

On the last and greatest day of the feast of Tabernacles, Jesus stood and cried out, "If anyone thirsts, let him come to Me and drink. He who believes in Me, as the Scripture has said, out of his heart will flow rivers of living water" (John 7:37-38). John explained that Jesus was speaking of the Holy Spirit, who should be received by believers, but was not yet given because Jesus had not yet been glorified (John 7:39). Wanting more of God is a requirement for receiving the Holy Spirit. We must go to Jesus to be filled; He is the One who baptizes in the Holy Spirit. If you are a believer of Jesus Christ and thirst for more of God in your life, you qualify as a candidate for the baptism of the Holy Spirit.

Placing your trust in the finished work of the cross of Jesus Christ signifies that you know you are a sinner, poor in spirit. You mourn for your sins and are saved when you confess Jesus Christ as your Lord and Savior. Once you are truly born again, you spiritually become a newborn babe in Christ. If you are alive and healthy, you hunger for food and thirst for water to grow. This is the case in our spiritual lives as well.

Peter said, "As newborn babes, desire the pure milk of the Word that you may grow thereby" (1 Peter 2:2). Thirst for more of God qualifies a believer for the "flow of living water": baptism in the Holy Spirit. If you are feeling unsatisfied with your Christian life, and something within tells you that there has got to be more to Christ than what you already have and know, then the Holy Spirit is wooing you. He is working to get you to a higher level of experience with God. This is God's desire. If you desire to have more of God in your life, then you should have no problem receiving the baptism of the Holy Spirit and being able to pray in tongues.

The apostle John told us that those who believed in Jesus during the feast could not receive the Holy Spirit then because the Holy Spirit had not yet been given—Jesus had not been glorified. After Jesus was glorified, the Holy Spirit was given on the day of Pentecost (John 12:16). Everyone waiting with Peter and the other apostles received the Holy Spirit on that day; they all spoke in tongues.

Ask to be filled with the Holy Spirit

Even though Jesus said that the river of living water, or the Holy Spirit, would flow from the heart of every thirsty believer, each believer still must ask to receive.

> So I say to you, ask, and it will be given to you; seek, and you will find; knock, and it will be opened to you. For everyone who asks, receives; and he who seeks, finds; and to him who knocks, it will be opened. If a

son asks for bread from any father among you, will he give him a stone? Or if he asks for a fish, will he give him a serpent instead of a fish? Or if he asks for an egg, will he offer him a scorpion? If you then, being evil, know how to give good gifts to your children, how much more will your heavenly Father give the Holy Spirit to those who ask Him!

—Luke 11:9-13

John the Baptist and every minister of the gospel baptize with water, but Jesus baptizes with the Holy Spirit, so believers must go to Him and ask to be baptized. Jesus refuses no one. Jesus said, "All that the Father gives Me will come to Me, and the one who comes to Me I will by no means cast out" (John 6:37).

Jesus spoke much about asking, and assured us in every way that we would receive if we only asked. That should have been enough for us, considering the nature of the One who spoke those words, but He went further, because some people have a way of excluding themselves from everything that is good, believing that they are not worthy to receive. Jesus said, "Everyone who asks receives." "Everyone" means you. "Everyone" means me. No one is turned away. There are no conditions for asking; you only need to be born again. There is no promise more reassuring than this. All you have to do to receive the Holy Spirit, according to Jesus, is to ask. How difficult could that be? Just ask! James supported this by saying that we do not have because we do not ask (James 4:2).

Jesus said, "If a son asks for bread from any father among you, will he give him a stone? Or if he asks for a fish, will he give him a serpent instead of a fish? Or if he asks for an egg, will he offer him a scorpion?" (Luke 11:11-12). Notice that everything the son asks for is something to eat—bread, fish, an egg—and everything that the father will not offer, according to Jesus, are things that would harm the child—a stone, a serpent, a scorpion. Jesus assured us that earthly fathers will not offer evil things to their children when they are asking for food; likewise, God will never offer us anything that would harm us.

Some Christians who are fearful of Satan's ability to deceive worry that they may not be worthy of receiving the Holy Spirit, and that Satan could use the occasion of their asking to fill them with a demonic spirit instead. Are only holy men worthy of receiving the Holy Spirit? But can a man be truly holy without the Holy Spirit? The Holy Spirit fills men who are not holy and makes them holy and acceptable before God. A man who knows he is unholy, yet wants to be holy before God, is a good candidate for receiving the Holy Spirit. God will not deny a Christian who is asking to receive something that will provide him with the "nutrients" necessary for spiritual growth.

Let us say that a child is hungry and asks his father for bread, and that the father replies, "Son, you know we have much bread, but could you just wait until next week, when I know you will be really desperate for bread? Then you can have all the bread you want!" Most fathers on earth would not do this—neither would our heavenly Father. You will receive as soon as you ask.

Jesus said, "If you then, being evil, know how to give good gifts to your children, how much more will your heavenly Father give the Holy Spirit to those who ask Him!" (Luke 11:13). Jesus is very specific about what He wants you to ask the Father for: the Holy Spirit. He assures you that you will receive Him when you ask. You do not have to wait. As a child of God, all you have to do to receive the Holy Spirit is ask.

Do not put on false humility. Do not say you are not worthy. No man is worthy. Do not try to believe—just believe! Jesus said we

 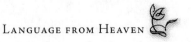

would be given the Holy Spirit. Do not look for a feeling as a sign that you have received what you asked for; Jesus did not say you would receive a "feeling." Jesus did not say, you will feel an electric current going through your body, or feel hot or cold, excited, or happy. If you have some of these feelings, enjoy them—but do not rely on them. Jesus said we would receive the Holy Spirit if we asked. We walk by faith and not by sight (2 Corinthians 5:7). Believe that His Word is good. This honors God.

What do I do after I have prayed to receive the Holy Spirit?

After you have prayed for the Holy Spirit, you should believe that God has given you the Holy Spirit and thank Him for blessing you, whether you feel something or not.

> Therefore I say to you, whatever things you ask when you pray, believe that you receive them, and you will have them.
>
> —Mark 11:24

After you have thanked Him, begin to speak in tongues. Do not say another word in your natural language once you truly believe that you have received. Faith in God's Word is your assurance, not feelings. Faith that God cannot lie is what assures you. This pleases God!

Being slain in the spirit is another supernatural work of God in which the Spirit freezes your motor skills as He does some deep work inside you, and you fall to the ground. Being slain in the Spirit and speaking in tongues are two different events. They can occur together, but never settle for being slain in the spirit without speaking in tongues when you are asking God for the baptism of the Holy Spirit.

> And they were all filled with the Holy Spirit and began to speak with other tongues, as the Spirit gave them utterance.
>
> —Acts 2:4

Believers use different methods to assist one who wants to be filled with the Holy Spirit. Sometimes seekers are told to praise God until their words change into tongues. This can be a very helpful method. It helps the believer express his faith in God through thanksgiving, but more importantly, the believer is speaking. You will not speak in tongues if your mouth is closed and you say nothing. The Holy Spirit will not speak in tongues for you. You must do the speaking—the Holy Spirit gives the utterance.

In chapter 2 of Acts, those who received the Holy Spirit on the day of Pentecost immediately began to speak with tongues. I personally believe that one who has prayed and believes that he or she has received the Holy Spirit should immediately begin to speak in tongues by faith. The believer must immediately step out of the boat and walk on water. Testing the water to see if it will hold your weight will keep you in the boat with unbelief. Believe the word of the Master and speak in tongues right after giving thanks in your language. Thanking God in your own native tongue is testimony that you are sure God has heard, and that you have received the Holy Spirit. After thanksgiving, step out in faith and begin to speak in tongues. If you believe you have received, then speak in tongues by faith.

By the grace of God, I have encouraged hundreds of people to receive the Holy Spirit in this way. Some of them are now ministers of the gospel in the United States and in Nigeria. Some were instantly healed and delivered from demonic oppression as they stepped out in faith to take what God had given to them.

> And from the days of John the Baptist until now the kingdom of heaven suffers violence, and the violent take it by force.
>
> —Matthew 11:12

If you receive anything from God, it will be by grace through faith. Faith is acting on the Word of God, which you believe with all your heart. If you cannot act on His Word, then the strength of your faith is questionable.

Get out of the boat and walk

Jesus told His disciples to get into a boat and go to the other side of the sea, but He went up by Himself up the mountain to pray. Later, he walked on the water to meet the disciples. When they saw Him, they were afraid, thinking He was a Ghost, but He assured them that He was the One. Then Peter said to Jesus, "Lord, if it is You, command me to come to You on the water" (Matthew 14:28). Jesus told him to come, and Peter stepped out of the boat and walked on water to the meet Jesus.

Peter walked on the water for some time, but he was not able to walk all the way to Jesus because he doubted, and began to sink because of unbelief. If he had tried the water to see if it would hold his weight, he certainly would not have stepped out of the boat in the first place. He stepped out of the boat immediately after Jesus said the word "come." He did not hesitate. "No one, having put his hand to the plow, and looking back, is fit for the kingdom of God" (Luke 9:62). We must never hesitate. We must act on His word just as Peter did when he stepped out of the boat.

In the same way, we should speak in tongues after we have prayed to receive the Holy Spirit. We should not try to speak in tongues—we should speak in tongues without fear or unbelief. If you have all kinds of questions in your heart and continue to wonder what to say, you are not stepping out of the boat. You are still testing the waters to see if they will hold your weight. 1 Corinthians 14:2 tells us that we cannot understand what we are saying in tongues, so why should it matter how we sound when we begin to speak in tongues by faith?

Children make sounds

When children learn how to talk in a language, they start by making sounds that make no sense. Da, da, da, da . . . na, na, na . . . They do not speak from a bank of memory in their heads. They just make sounds. They are never embarrassed by the sounds they make. To their parents, these are beautiful sounds coming from their beloved child. Before long, children are able to say words that can be understood, and after that, they speak their language fluently.

When we receive Christ as Savior, we start out as babies. One who has prayed to receive the Holy Spirit should immediately step out in faith by making sounds through the power of the Holy Spirit, just like a baby without being concerned about how they sound. Jesus said, "Unless you are converted and become as little children, you will by no means enter the kingdom of heaven" (Matthew 18:3). Be a child before God so that you may receive all

He has for you. Humble yourself before Him, trust in Him, and act on His word without fear—this is what it takes to become like a child in the kingdom of God.

Many times, seekers are too self-conscious about how they sound, or they feel they should not make any sound that is not from the Holy Spirit. In their minds, God will be displeased if they do. I do not think a believer could make a sound or say one word that was not from the Holy Spirit if he is stepping out in faith to speak in tongues after prayer. But would God indeed be angry if this happened, even if the words were spoken in sincerity as the believer sought God's Spirit to move in his life? I do not think so. Nevertheless, I will emphasize that a sincere believer seeking to speak in tongues after receiving the Holy Spirit never makes a wrong sound or says a wrong word.

God did not abandon us while we were in sin before we accepted His Son as Savior. He revealed Himself to us and saved us. I believe God will work with every believer who steps out in faith to receive the Holy Spirit with the evidence of tongues. There is no need to be afraid. He loves His children dearly. He saved them through the painful death of His only begotten Son. The moment you begin to speak in tongues, the Holy Spirit will take over. God is faithful to His Word. His Word cannot fail, and He will not fail anyone who acts in faith on His spoken word.

The waters of the sea held Peter's weight when he stepped out of the boat at the invitation of Jesus. He did not sink right after he stepped out of the boat to walk to Jesus. If he had started to sink, he would have held onto the boat and gotten back in it. He sank when he changed his mind because of what he saw and felt. A child of God who prays to receive the Holy Spirit cannot open his or her mouth in faith and speak words that the Holy Spirit did not give.

Every time a believer speaks in tongues, he enters a supernatural realm, and he does so by faith. The believer should step out in faith by speaking in tongues boldly and without fear. God stays true to His Word. Speaking in tongues is an act of faith—if it is not, then it is not of God. Step out of the boat and speak. Do as children do. They trust their parents' words and act on them. Remember that Jesus said that unless we become like children we will not enter into the kingdom of God (Matthew 18:3). That means we would not be able to enjoy all that God has freely given to us in Christ. Become like a child so that God can release His blessings into your life. Open your mouth wide and let Him fill it (Psalm 81:10). As you step out in faith, begin to speak in tongues and the Holy Spirit will give you a beautiful language from heaven—a pure language with which to call on the Lord with one accord (Zephaniah 3:9).

The Holy Spirit will not speak for you

Some who have asked to be filled with the Holy Spirit are frustrated because they tried to pray in tongues but were not able. They are waiting for the Holy Spirit to speak in tongues for them. The question is, who is doing the praying? If the Holy Spirit speaks in tongues for the believer, then the believer is doing nothing; the Holy Spirit is the one doing the praying. But the Holy Spirit has no need; it is the believer who has needs. The truth is that the Holy Spirit will not do the speaking for anyone. He gives the utterance, but the believer must speak with his own tongue and voice. The Holy Spirit does not have a natural tongue with which to speak—the believer does. The Holy Spirit assists with the supernatural.

I have often reasoned with these people who think the believer mustn't do anything but allow the Holy Spirit to do the speaking

 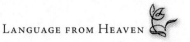

in tongues. They think the believer can speak in tongues only when the Holy Spirit wants to—in other words, that it is all up to the Holy Spirit. They think that if the Holy Spirit does not want to speak in tongues, the believer never will. If that were true, what would happen if the believer went to the grocery store, and at checkout, the cashier said, "Hi," and at that moment the Holy Spirit wanted to speak in tongues about something critical that demanded prayer? Would the believer then speak in tongues in reply to the cashier's greeting until the Holy Spirit quit, and then apologize to the cashier, saying, "It was the Holy Spirit"? That would be ridiculous! The spirit of the prophet is subject to the prophet (1 Corinthians 14:32). We do the speaking, and the Holy Spirit gives the utterance.

One thing that we must understand is that the Holy Spirit's job is to assist our spirits in prayer by helping our spirits to utter words in tongues. Some believe that when they speak in tongues, the Holy Spirit is the one praying. But Paul told us that it is our spirits doing the praying.

> For if I pray in a tongue, my spirit prays, but my understanding is unfruitful. What is the conclusion then? I will pray with the spirit, and I will also pray with the understanding. I will sing with the spirit, and I will also sing with the understanding.
> —1 Corinthians 14:14-15

The word "spirit" in 1 Corinthians 14:14 is lowercased, meaning it refers to the human spirit, not the Holy Spirit. Paul did not say that when he prays in tongues, the Holy Spirit prays. The Holy Spirit is actively involved, but it is Paul's spirit doing the praying. It is clear, then, that if we are unwilling to open our mouths to pray, we will not speak in tongues. One great lesson of this passage is that praying can be done in tongues. We have a say in how we want to pray: in tongues or with our understanding. I personally prefer tongues, because it is supernatural.

The will of the believer plays the major role

God never forces anyone to do anything. He speaks to us to persuade us to change our ways and follow His. He tells us the benefits of obeying Him and the consequences of not listening. Nevertheless, it is up to us to choose what we want to do. It is up to us to step out in faith to speak in tongues after we have asked Him to fill us with the Holy Spirit. If you refuse to make sounds with your mouth, you may never speak in tongues.

Many people are afraid of the unknown. You will never know or enjoy the unknown until you are willing to trust God for the outcome. The Bible tells us that if we are willing and obedient, we will eat of the good of the land (Isaiah 1:19). There is goodness in the land. We only enjoy all of God's blessings if we are willing, and then act on His word without fear, knowing He who promised is faithful (Hebrew 10:23).

Seeking the Holy Spirit

In the early 1980s, I began to ponder Scriptures concerning the Holy Spirit in light of what I was hearing in the church community. People talked about seeking the Holy Spirit. I began to wonder why we needed to seek Him. He is not lost—we are. He came to seek us. But after I was saved in 1975, I was instructed to seek

Him. So I sought the Holy Spirit for a long time. I often woke up early to seek the Spirit. I was satisfied with seeking Him for a long time without result. Seeking Him felt good, even though I came away without the gift each time. I was seeking the Holy Spirit!

I wondered occasionally in those days when I would know for sure that I had sought Him enough and had received, and that it was time to begin speaking in tongues. Even though I was satisfied to be a seeker of the Holy Spirit, I was frustrated because no one told me how I was to know when I had received. God was merciful to me, and one day I spoke in tongues. I began to question why believers were being told to go on seeking the Holy Spirit. I felt that this instruction left the seeker with uncertainty about when to release faith to receive the gift. I did not know it then, but now I know it was God prompting me to study the subject so I could be of help to those who sincerely want the gift. I began to study the subject with prayer.

Through God, I gained much information on the subject. Finally, I decided to act on what God had shown me. He instructed me to encourage believers seeking to be baptized in the Holy Spirit to begin to speak in tongues right after they had asked to be filled. They must receive by faith, not by bombarding the throne of God with their requests. After they had prayed to receive the Spirit, I was to ask them to believe that they had received, and to join me immediately in speaking in tongues. They were not to try to repeat what I was saying in tongues, but by faith to join me. I was unsure of this practice at first. This was not what I had been taught, but I felt I had to put the information I had obtained by revelation into practice.

I had my first opportunity to do so at a night vigil. I boldly proclaimed before those in the meeting that I could help sincere seekers to receive the Holy Spirit. Many in that meeting were unsure of my newfound revelation and my boldness, and were unwilling to ask for help. They had not seen me in this light before and did not know how to respond. However, one person in the crowd was willing to give it a try. I think this woman had been desperate and could have cared less who prayed for her. I shared with her from the Scriptures, showing her what God had shown to me. She understood me well, and as we prayed, she told me she felt electrical currents going through her body—but she did not speak in tongues. I was not satisfied with her experience of "electrical currents"! I wanted her to speak in tongues. I had separated her from everyone else in the room and taken her to another room in our church. Those in the next room were waiting to hear what transpired, what God had done, and a testimony about feeling electrical currents would not satisfy them. I did all I could to encourage her to step out in faith and pray in tongues, but she did not.

She assured me that she had gotten the message, and that she would start all over again when she got back to her dormitory at the University of Georgia. When I heard this, I was comforted. I knew she had indeed gotten the message, and that she will be filled with the Holy Spirit. We left the room and joined the others. They waited for some time to hear from us, but we said nothing. Then someone asked her pointedly what had happened. She replied that she had felt "electricity." Everyone laughed, and the joke was on me for stepping out in boldness without result. Nevertheless, before we left on the morning after the prayer meeting, she came to comfort me, telling me not to worry because she had the message down in her heart.

When I got back home that morning, I had a hard time going to sleep. I kept waiting for the phone to ring. I was waiting for her call. I waited, and then drifted into deep sleep. Then, right after twelve o'clock noon, the phone rang. I knew it was her calling. I jumped and ran to the phone, and it was her on the other end. She was talking so excitedly I could not understand what she was saying. I told her to calm down. She did, and then she told me what I had been waiting all morning to hear. She could speak in tongues fluently, and she was filled with much joy.

I have since been able to help hundreds receive the gift of the Holy Spirit by faith. They have spoken in tongues as I encouraged them to join me by faith. On some occasions, over a hundred people received at the same time. Many of them were people who had just been saved at a crusade meeting I had just conducted. It was easy to help these new believers receive the Holy Spirit. They were like clean slates. No one had told them they could not receive. They spoke in tongues boldly. Some of those I helped years ago are now effective ministers of the gospel today. I believe thousands could receive at once through what God showed me if they just were present at the same meeting.

CHAPTER 11

USING THE GIFT

You can speak in tongues whenever you want

Once you have received the Holy Spirit and have spoken in tongues, you have received your prayer language. You can pray in tongues whenever you want. It is your gift, and you can use it whenever you want to.

> For if I pray in a tongue, my spirit prays, but my understanding is unfruitful. What is the conclusion then? I will pray with the spirit, and I will also pray with the understanding. I will sing with the spirit, and I will also sing with the understanding.
> —1 Corinthians 14:14-15

Some Christians only pray in tongues when they are emotionally stimulated during a service. Usually they say a few words in tongues and then quit. They feel good about it, and claim it was a good service because they were moved to speak in tongues a little bit.

However, the real speaking in tongues, according to Paul, should be done elsewhere, not during a church service. You can pray with the spirit and you can pray with understanding as well. You can pray in the spirit as long as you want, and you can also pray with understanding as long as you want. It is your spirit. You must do the praying. You can sing with the sprit in tongues, and you can sing with the understanding, too. The decision is yours.

When you pray in tongues, your spirit is edified, but you mind is not, because you do not understand the words you are saying in tongues. When you pray with the understanding, your mind is edified. Praying with understanding is good, but it is only natural, not supernatural. Praying in tongues is supernatural. I believe praying in tongues is more helpful than praying with the understanding for getting the believer more in tune with the Holy Spirit. There is nothing wrong with praying with the understanding; it just doesn't do as much good for the believer spiritually. The Holy Spirit is actively engaged when we pray in tongues, and He is God. Praying in tongues energizes our lives in secret as we pray to God in the spirit. The power is seen in our public walk, both inside and outside of the church.

In the Scriptures, believers are often encouraged to pray in the spirit (Ephesians 6:18; Jude 1:20). To pray in the spirit, you must pray in tongues. Many pray more often in their natural languages than in tongues. They have the supernatural ability to reach God by praying in tongues, but somehow they feel better praying more in natural language. Could this be due to some form of deception from the Devil, or a decision based on fear of the unknown? Praying in tongues takes you from the natural realm into the supernatural one. Paul said, "I will pray with the spirit, and I will also pray with the understanding" (1 Corinthians 14:15). Paul decided to pray with the spirit and with the understanding, also. He did both, and both benefitted him spiritually. Following his example would spiritually benefit us today.

Why is it that Christians prefer to pray primarily with the understanding? Believers would grow more rapidly in faith and in the knowledge of God if they spent more time praying in the spirit. Speaking in tongues is supernatural, and it carries the one doing so into the supernatural realm of the Spirit. God is Spirit and wants us to worship Him in spirit and in truth.

How I pray

I realized that when I pray in the spirit, my mind can wander all over the place if it is not truly engaged in prayer. When you pray in tongues, your spirit is engaged, but your mind does not understand what you are saying in the spirit, so it is not engaged. Because the mind is not engaged while we are praying in tongues, the mind wanders. We must engage it in prayer also. What I started doing to solve this problem is praying with both my spirit and my mind at the same time. My mind is engaged in prayer while I am praying in tongues. It was a wonderful discovery for me, and has been a great source of blessing to my life in every way.

You have control

Paul said the spirit of a prophet is subject to the prophet (1 Corinthians 14:32). You have control. You can choose to speak in tongues for a short time or a long time. It is really up to you. You can stop at any time. Some have received the Holy Spirit, spoken in tongues during a service, and not spoken in tongues since. They

were moved emotionally during the service, perhaps during the song service or when they were prayed for at the altar to receive the Holy Spirit, but they have not said a word in tongues since. They have become fearful and doubtful of what they received. They know to stay with God, but they want to forget that they once spoke in tongues. Some of these people have become uncomfortable around those who pray in tongues regularly. Some have moved to churches where nothing about speaking in tongues is mentioned. They have settled on living the Christian life in a way that is comfortable to them, apart from what God has shown them. However, comfort is not the important thing in this matter. What matters most is what God says and what He wants from us.

The will of God, according to the Word of God, is most important for all true believers. Do we ignore His Word and what He has shown us, and live according to what makes sense to us rather than according to what the Scriptures teach? Should every child of God not seek the best of what the Father offers? If you have received the Holy Spirit sometime in the past, you can still pray in tongues today. It is really up to you. If you believe you did not live right before God after you received the Holy Spirit, but you want to draw closer to Him today, all you have to do is confess your sins before God and receive forgiveness by faith in the blood of Jesus. After you have done this, you may pray in tongues again, just like before. The gifts and calling of God are irrevocable (Romans 11:29).

One possible reason why some stop praying in tongues is that they are waiting to experience again that feeling they had when they received the Holy Spirit and spoke in tongues for the very first time. They are waiting for a feeling to give them the cue to speak in tongues. However, this is not how it works. Speaking in tongues is an act of faith. We walk by faith and not by sight or feelings

(2 Corinthians 5:7). You can exercise your faith by speaking in tongues. The benefits are great.

In 1988, I was ministering at a church service in Nigeria, and had just prayed with about thirty people to receive the Holy Spirit. Many of them received and began to pray in tongues loudly. I walked among them to help those who were dealing with unbelief and were not able to receive. Eventually, almost everyone who came forward to receive was speaking in tongues. I wanted to give them further instruction about the gift they had received, so I asked everyone to stop. I knew they had control.

Everyone stopped except for one lady. I pleaded with her to stop, but she did not. Then I said to her, "One who is filled with the Spirit of God has control and can stop at any time. If you cannot stop, then we will have to start casting out a devil." She immediately stopped speaking in tongues. I knew she had received the Holy Spirit and had control over the tongues she spoke, but she wanted all to know she had the gift. You can speak in tongues as long as you want; it is your gift from the Father. Use your prayer language to advance yourself in matters of faith. Do not neglect the gift.

My mother received the Holy Spirit

My mother initially rejected my faith in the Lord Jesus Christ and gave me trouble about it in the first two years after I was saved. She eventually accepted Christ, primarily because I stopped preaching at her and showed her love and respect. Mama was already saved when I went back home after graduating from the University of Georgia with a master's degree in science. My plan was to return to the United States to continue my studies, so I spent my time in

 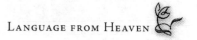

Nigeria preaching and praying for people. When it became known to the believers in town that I could help them receive the Holy Spirit, a steady flow of people came to our home to receive. All I did was to share the truth about the Holy Spirit and encourage them to step out in faith by speaking in tongues. Mama watched many come and leave with joy because they had received the Holy Spirit. I believe some of them shared with her about what had happened to them. Mama attended a church that did not believe in speaking in tongues, and I did not want to pressure her to pray for the gift. I am sure she heard me as I instructed others on the subject.

My practice during that year in Nigeria was to wake up early to spend at least one hour praying, and I did most of it in tongues. One morning, mama slipped into my room during my prayer time, and sat down. I was surprised by that, and wondered what the matter was. She said to me in a very serious tone, "Son, did I offend you?" We had gone to bed the previous night with no incident and we had been very happy in our relationship as mother and son, so I was confused.

I asked her why she was asking a strange question like that when we had not had a single disagreement in a very long time. She said that she had watched many come to me for prayer to receive the Holy Spirit, but that I had not once asked her whether she wanted to receive. I told her that I did not know that she wanted to receive. Her request blessed me greatly! I was filled with joy! We prayed together for her to receive the Holy Spirit, and she received, and began to speak with tongues. After that experience, mama joined me most mornings for our hour of prayer. Mama's life was transformed and she became a powerful witness for Christ, full of the love of Jesus.

The tongues are not of God

It is important that I address the question of doubt. Many Christians, after they have been filled with the Holy Spirit, soon begin to feel like something is not right. They begin to wonder whether the tongues they are speaking are from the Holy Spirit. Some feel that their prayer was just them making silly sounds, and not the Holy Spirit. Their experience does not match what they had previously envisioned the baptism of the Holy Spirit to be.

One lady called to inform me that she was going to stop speaking in tongues altogether. She informed me that she was repeating the same word over and over again and that she had become very familiar with that word. She felt foolish repeating the same word over and over again. She noted that others spoke many words in the spirit, but she spoke just one word. I asked her if she could change to another word, as she spoke in tongues by her own will. She said that that was the problem: she could not. It always stayed the same. Then I told her the fact that she would have loved to change from repeating that one word to speaking more words in the Spirit told me that the Holy Spirit was involved in what she was doing. The Spirit gives utterance to what we are saying in the Spirit. If He wants us to say something to the Father in tongues, and He knows all things, we should let Him lead. This lady accepted my counsel, and before long began to pray with tongues using many words. We must do the speaking, but what we say when we speak in tongues is up to the Holy Spirit. We speak in tongues trusting in the goodness of God, the grace of our Lord Jesus Christ, and the power of the Holy Spirit to guide us into all truth.

Many Christians quit speaking in tongues because of their doubt. Questioning what one has received from God is a major trick of the devil. Many Christians struggle with whether they are saved or not long after they receive Christ as Savior. The Devil tells them that they are not truly saved. A man who cares nothing about God, Christ, or the Holy Spirit does not walk the streets wondering whether he is saved or not; God is not in his thoughts. However, Satan harasses those who have been truly saved with lies, telling them that they have not been saved. Well, the Devil is unable to speak truth, so if he is telling you that you are not, then you must truly be saved. Glory to God!

The Devil lies to believers all around the world about speaking in tongues. He truly fears this gift! He does not want Christians to become as children, accepting the Word of God as Jesus recommended (Matthew 18:3). When believers are willing to accept God's Word enough to act on it, Satan injects doubt and fear. Some fear that speaking in tongues is of the Devil, not of God. If they have not studied the Scriptures on this subject, fear and doubt reign. They feel better playing it safe. However, ignorance could lead to missed opportunities in life to really be used of God. The Bible says that God's people have gone into captivity because they have no knowledge (Isaiah 5:13). The Devil does not just sit back when you ignore God's Word; he seeks to take you into captivity and to keep you there.

"From the days of John the Baptist until now the kingdom of God suffers violence, and the violent ones take it by force" (Matthew 11:12). We do not force God's hand to receive things from Him. He has given all willingly and freely through our Lord Jesus Christ. Our battle is with our archenemy, the Devil, who does not want us to receive all that God has given. He wants to keep us from the truth. His tactics have not changed. Just as he questioned God's instruction to Adam and Eve concerning the Tree of the knowledge of Good and Evil, he questions God's Word concerning the baptism of the Holy Spirit. Many accept his lies and avoid this precious gift for which Jesus died to give believers. His death took away our sins, and paved the way for us to be filled with the Holy Spirit. Knowledge of the truth sets us free. Knowledge is power, and revelation of the Word of God is supernatural power.

The Devil also lies about those who have received the baptism of the Holy Spirit. He tells stories which make them appear strange and odd. Strange things may happen to those who speak in tongues, but that does not change the fact that the doctrine is biblical. As men reach out to God, mistakes are made, but the one in control is God, not man. Paul said that he was confident of this very thing, that He who has begun a good work in you will complete it until the day of Jesus Christ (Philippians 1:6). God is the One who began the work, and at the beginning, nothing is perfect. However, God does not give up on anything. He perfects His work.

The Devil sometimes challenges many who received the Holy Spirit by telling them that the tongues they speak actually came from him, the Devil. When his lies are believed, the believer stops using his prayer language. He starts to pray only with the understanding, and in so doing, misses out on the power of the Holy Spirit resident in Him. The Devil has done everything to prevent believers from receiving the Holy Spirit. However, he is no match for the Holy Spirit. Many around the world have been filled with the Holy Spirit. Many people in third world countries have embraced the power of the Holy Spirit by speaking in tongues. They believe in the power of the Holy Spirit, and God confirms their faith by giving them signs (Mark 16:20).

Do not believe Satan's lies. Continue to pray in tongues often. Spend lengthy sessions with the Holy Spirit in your prayer life. If the Devil makes you feel like the tongues you are speaking are not from the Holy Spirit, do not quit. If you continue in prayer, the feeling will leave you, and faith will arise in your soul. There is no better way of dealing with unbelief than spending quality time before God speaking and praying in tongues.

Sometimes the Devil lies to those who have received the Holy Spirit by telling them that the tongues cannot be of God because the prayer sounds just like the believers themselves. Well, if it does not sound like you, who would it sound like? It should not sound like Jesus. You are not Jesus. It should sound like you. If it does not, then we are dealing with a demon. Your prayer must be in your voice. It must sound like you; you are the one praying. The Holy Spirit is the Helper. His job is to add the supernatural element to your prayer by enabling you to pray in a language that you did not learn and cannot understand unless the Holy Spirit chooses to give you the meaning (1 Corinthians 14:2, 13).

Speaking in tongues is for everyone

My Christian life took a turn for the better not on the day I received the Holy Spirit, but when I decided that regardless of how I felt, I was going to pray in tongues for as long as I could each day. When we pray in tongues, we call on the Lord with the pure language from heaven (Zephaniah 3:9). This is what puts peace, rest and refreshing into the hearts of the weary (Isaiah 28:12). Speaking in tongues will help your faith to grow tremendously (Jude 1:20). Speaking in tongues is for all believers. The gift was never intended for a select few, but for all who believe (John 7:35). Jesus said that our heavenly Father will give the Holy Spirit to all who ask (Luke 11:13). I do not follow the doctrines of a specific church denomination, but what I believe in is what the Bible teaches. The message of speaking in tongues did not come from

Pentecostal or Charismatic believers, but from the Bible. So the message of speaking in tongues is not just for a specific Christian denomination, but for all believers. It behooves every believer to search the Scriptures carefully for the truths they contain, because in them, we find God.

Why don't you bow your head now and pray to God? If you do not know Christ as your personal Savior, ask Him to come into your heart. Ask him to forgive your sins. If you ask, you will receive forgiveness. Then, ask Him to fill you with the Holy Spirit (Luke 11:9-13). There is no set time between one's salvation and receiving the Holy Spirit. You may have been saved years ago, or maybe you were saved yesterday. It really does not matter. What matters is that you ask to receive the Holy Spirit. Everyone who asks receives, Jesus told us (Matthew 7:8). If you ask, God, who cannot lie, will give you the Holy Spirit.

After you have asked Him, believe that you have received, because you know God does not turn His back on His Word. Thank Him from the bottom of your heart for the gift of the Holy Spirit. Take your time in thanking Him. Now you must stop thanking Him in your language; do not say another word in your language. Start speaking in tongues. Continue in thanksgiving, but do so in tongues. You must do the speaking. You must make the sounds with your mouth. God will not do that for you. The Holy Spirit will give the utterance. He is quick to confirm God's word. He will not allow you to say one word that does not come from the Spirit of God. Do not try to speak in tongues; speak. After you prayed to receive, you were baptized in the Holy Spirit, whether you felt something or not. Feelings have nothing to do with it. We must stand on His Word, not our feelings.

John the Baptist baptized all who came to him. Jesus can certainly do better than John. He will baptize with the Holy Spirit all who come to Him. He will not refuse anyone! Do not focus on how you sound as you speak in tongues. Your words are beautiful in the Father's ears, regardless of how you think you sound. He understands everything you are saying.

Do not whisper in tongues at this time. You must hear yourself speak. Take deep breaths and speak with reckless abandon. Speak as loud as you are comfortable with. "God has not given us a spirit of fear, but of power and of love and of a sound mind" (2 Timothy 1:7). Speaking in tongues is supernatural. It is the pure language from heaven. God gave us tongues to call on His name with one accord. Paul told us to pray "always with all prayer and supplication in the Spirit, being watchful to this end with all perseverance and supplication for all the saints" (Ephesians 6:18). Pray for all of God's people, and do so in the spirit, in tongues. May the Lord show you great and mighty things as you continue with your discovery in Him with the help of His Holy Spirit in you, Amen!

CHAPTER 12

A WORLD OF DISCOVERY

Now that you have received the Holy Spirit and can pray in your prayer language, spend a lot of time praying in tongues every day. This is the gateway to understanding the mysteries of the kingdom of God. This, I believe, is the reason God gave us tongues to communicate with Him in the realm of the supernatural.

The Bible is the manual for successful living, but the truths in it are shrouded in mysteries. To unlock the mysteries, we need prayer. Praying with the help of our divine Helper, the Holy Spirit, is the only sure way to unlock the truths hidden in the Bible. Jesus said, "You shall know the truth and the truth will make you free" (John 8:32). This means that you remain bound until you discover the truth. Revelation is the discovery of the truths hidden in the Word of God. Once we obtain the truth from His word, we have the benefit of them.

> The secret things belong to the Lord our God, but those things which are revealed belong to us and to our children forever, that we may do all the words of this law.
>
> —Deuteronomy 29:29

Whatever God has chosen to keep secret must be left to God. Man will never benefit from what God does not want him to know. It is futile to seek to know what God does not want to reveal to man. For example, God has chosen not to make known to man the date of the return of our Lord Jesus Christ. Seeking to know will only give the seeker and those who follow his example confusion and embarrassment. Jesus said, "It is not for you to know the times or seasons which the Father has put in His own authority" (Acts 1:7). However, as the great and loving Father, there is much that He wants to reveal to His children for their benefit. Revelation comes through the Holy Spirit, given to man as his ultimate Helper.

Truth and the natural man

A natural man is the man who has not received Christ as Lord and Savior. He is not born again. He does not have the Spirit of God living inside him. He is not spiritual. What God says in His Word sometimes goes against the way the man sees and understands things. Therefore, he rejects truths from the Word of God that could bring him deliverance, peace, and a wonderful relationship with the Father. How truly sad! The natural man cannot understand truths in the Scriptures. They seem foolish to him. It takes the involvement of the Holy Spirit for a man to be able to fully grasp the truths of God.

> But the natural man does not receive the things of the Spirit of God, for they are foolishness to him; nor can he know them, because they are spiritually discerned.
> —1 Corinthians 2:14

The Word of God is supernatural. The Bible tells us that the Word of God is God (John 1:1). The Word became flesh and dwelt among us in the person of Jesus. It is clear that the word of God is not ordinary. The Word of God is divine. It is not natural, so a natural man cannot truly understand what the Word says. God's Word can only be truly discerned through the power of the Holy Spirit. It should not bother Christians when people speak against the word of God and against Christians for what they believe. They speak from their limited understanding, which is only natural. Christians cannot make people who are not true believers accept what the Word says. This can only be done through the power of the Holy Spirit. Similarly, a Christian who is not baptized with the Holy Spirit may be able to understand basic truths in the Scriptures, but when it comes to the supernatural acts of God in signs and wonders, barriers prevents the believer from accepting and acting on the word.

Praying in tongues is supernatural

Many Christians are running all over the place looking for the supernatural. Some of these people are truly gullible because they do not know the Scriptures. Some become a bit weird as they subscribe to acts and beliefs that are not truly Scriptural. Many have been offered the true gate into the supernatural things of God, but because they lack true understanding, they still feel inadequate. The baptism of the Holy Spirit is the door to everything that is truly divine and supernatural. Praying in tongues is supernatural! When you speak in tongues, you immediately step out of the natural into the supernatural realm, from the fleshly into the spirit realm. When you speak in tongues, you are ushered into the realm

LANGUAGE FROM HEAVEN

where signs and wonders take place. Praying in tongues is holy. It is of God. It is biblical.

Praying in tongues gives us the spiritual discernment we need to unlock the mysteries hidden in the Word of God. We must not allow anyone or anything to stop us from using our prayer language to communicate with God. It is one of the most precious gifts from the Lord to the church of our Lord Jesus Christ. This supernatural gift lifts us up to the heavenly realm where we can obtain all the spiritual blessings God has for us.

> Blessed be the God and Father of our Lord Jesus Christ, who has blessed us with every spiritual blessing in the heavenly places in Christ.
>
> —Ephesians 1:3

I believe that as you spend time praying in tongues, you receive the spirit of wisdom and revelation in the knowledge of Him, the eyes of your understanding are enlightened, and you know the hope of His calling, the riches of the glory of God's inheritance in the saints, and the exceeding greatness of His power toward us who believe (Ephesians 1:17-19).

The fact that Paul never ceased to pray for the Ephesian Christians in this way is a clear indication that spiritual wisdom and understanding that comes with enlightenment are critical with regards to living the Christian life. Spiritual knowledge of who we are in Him, what He has accomplished on our behalves, the power that is at work in us, and our place in God will put the Devil in a constant defensive posture as we act on what we know. We will then be able to recognize his lies, resist him strongly, and watch him flee from us in terror.

The Bible is a book of wonders. It is the road map for living. Although it is written in a language all who speak the language can understand, the message in it can only be fully grasped with the help of the Holy Spirit. The truths contained within are holy and heavenly, but they have significant influence on successful living on the earth. Jesus said the Word of God contains the mysteries of the kingdom of heaven. The Holy Spirit of God came from heaven and is an integral part of the mysteries of the kingdom of God. The Spirit has been given to us to help us unlock these hidden truths in the Word of God. The mysteries are for our benefit, but we must first unlock them before we can enjoy them.

It is sad to know that some of God's children are still natural. Their spiritual understanding has remained the same from the day they were born again. Some do not even seem to care. They have no desire for more of God. Receiving Christ for them is like obtaining a ticket to get into heaven. Obtaining the ticket is satisfying enough for them. The deed is done, and that is it. No thought is given to making a heartfelt commitment to the One who gave all to make heaven possible for us. They have no real desire to know more about the Savior. Nothing in their lives is supernatural. They only turn to God when things are somewhat difficult, relying on others to communicate with the heavenly Father for deliverance. However, serving God is more than just accepting Christ as Lord as Savior. God wants us to grow in the knowledge of Him. The believer has got to have a personal relationship with God. The believer must make every effort to get to know Him better. Knowing Him better comes to us by revelation.

If a living thing is not growing, then it is in the process of dying. This can happen to our relationship with God also. Jesus said, "He who overcomes shall be clothed in white garments, and I will not blot out his name from the Book of Life; but I will confess his name before My Father and before His angels" (Revelation 3:5). Will Jesus actually blot out the names of a Christian who have not overcome? That is exactly what He said He would do, and He is not a liar. His word will not return to Him void (Isaiah 55:11). Jesus also threatened to vomit certain believers out of His mouth. "I know your works, that you are neither cold nor hot. I could wish you were cold or hot. So then, because you are lukewarm, and neither cold nor hot, I will vomit you out of My mouth" (Revelation 3:15-16). Christians need to hunger and thirst for righteousness. There is always a need for more of God in our lives. If you are satisfied with your Christian growth and lose your desire to have more of God, chances are that you are on your way down from the grace of God. It is hard to live the Christian life without God's grace. Praying in tongues consistently before God will put the fire in your spirit to keep you current with what the Spirit is saying (Revelation 3:22). The writer of the book of Hebrews warned us to look out so we wouldn't fall short of the grace of God (Hebrews 12:15). We cannot live the Christian life without the grace of God. We cannot fight spiritual battles with mental weapons; we need spiritual weapons.

We must keep the flames of our love for Him burning. The Holy Spirit has been given to us to make this happen. We cannot depend on our own abilities. We cannot lean on our own understanding, or on how we feel (Proverb 3:5). We cannot rely on our past exploits in God. We must put the past—good or bad—behind us, and stay focused on pressing hard after God (Philippians 3:13-14). Remember that our strength and wisdom without Him are never enough to carry us through the troubles of life.

> "Not by might nor by power, but by My Spirit," Says the Lord of hosts.
>
> —Zechariah 4:6

Hunger for more of God

Hungering for more of God always yields pleasant results in the life of the believer. If you are a believer and you find yourself wanting more of God, then you are blessed! The hunger in you will be filled (Matthew 5:6). As you pursue more of God, I believe that God will lead you into the baptism of the Holy Spirit with speaking in tongues just like He did with Cornelius in chapter 10 of the book of Acts. Cornelius was a Roman Centurion who loved God and was very devoted to Him. He and his household feared God and gave alms generously. He prayed to God always. He wanted more of God, and for that reason, God sent an angel to Cornelius in a vision. God's message was for Cornelius to send for a man called Peter. Cornelius' hunger for God caused the Lord to send an angel so that Cornelius and his family and friends could hear the gospel and be filled with the Holy Spirit. God gave Cornelius a greater anointing of the Holy Spirit in his life. This is usually God's answer to a heart that desires more of Him. All in Cornelius' home were filled with the Holy Spirit and spoke in tongues (Acts 10:44-46).

If you are a Christian but you do not hunger for more of God or desire to be in His presence, you should be concerned. That is not a good place to be. Every believer must strive to keep his relationship with God alive and on fire; he must always want more of God. For a believer not to desire to be in the house of God, the presence of God, or fellowship with other believers is spiritually dangerous. "Now the just shall live by faith; but if anyone draws back, My soul has no pleasure in him" (Hebrews 10:38).

Baptism in the Holy Spirit will not cause the hunger in you to cease, but to intensify. As you seek God with your prayer language, you will begin to understand more and more about God, the Devil, the kingdom of God, and the reason that Christ came. The more

LANGUAGE FROM HEAVEN

you understand, the more of God you will want in your life. You become more effective as a kingdom worker. Then you will begin to shine like a light to those around you.

Being baptized in the Holy Spirit with the ability to speak in tongues is the doorway to a world of discovery of God's mysteries. God has prepared things for those who love Him (1 Corinthians 2:9), but His beloved children cannot enjoy them until they know what they are. Many criticize what they do not fully understand; they sometimes call these false doctrines. They take neither the time to search for these things for themselves in the Scriptures, nor the time to ask the Holy Spirit to give them understanding. Some of these people are carnal Christians; they are not walking according to the Spirit, but trying to understand spiritual truths with their natural minds, fighting spiritual battles with mental weapons.

> But the natural man does not receive the things of the
> Spirit of God, for they are foolishness to him; nor can
> he know them, because they are spiritually discerned.
> —1 Corinthians 2:14

The place of knowledge

There are great treasures hidden in the word of God. But we cannot enjoy them until we discover them. This is why Paul prayed ceaselessly for the Ephesian believers to be given the Spirit of wisdom and revelation in the knowledge of God (Ephesians 1:15--23). His desire for them was for them to know. Knowing is what ushers in the fulfillment of the promises of God.

Peter told us that grace and peace are multiplied in our lives only according to the knowledge of God and our Lord Jesus Christ

(2 Peter 1:2). He also told us that God has given us exceedingly great and precious promises, and through these promises, we may partake of His divine nature (2 Peter 1:4). However, we cannot enjoy the blessing of these promises until we know and believe them. The Bible tells us that it is impossible to please God without faith. Faith in God's promise is the only thing that causes God to respond. The Holy Spirit is the One who searches out these deep secrets of God, and in prayer He reveals them to us (1 Corinthians 2:10-12). As He reveals them to us, faith to receive them is born in our hearts or spirits.

God does want all mankind to partake of His divine nature. This was His plan from the beginning. God said, "Let Us make man in Our image, according to Our likeness; let them have dominion over the fish of the sea, over the birds of the air, and over the cattle, over all the earth and over every creeping thing that creeps on the earth" (Genesis 1:26). God wanted man to partake of His divine nature while living on the earth. That plan has not changed. However, to partake, we must have knowledge. Divine knowledge is given to us only through the Holy Spirit. We must seek revelation from God. We must seek to be enlightened in the Word of God through the power of the Holy Spirit. We cannot read or study the Word of God and gain divine revelation without the Holy Spirit. To change our situations and circumstances for the better, we need the Helper and Teacher, the Holy Spirit. To do this, we must engage the Holy Spirit in our Bible study and prayer life. In my opinion, this can only happen when we spend time praying in the Holy Spirit, spending time with God as we call on the name of the Lord and study His Word.

There are treasures in the Word of God that can change our lives for the better. We must search for these treasures with the help of the Holy Spirit. It is a life long search. There is much to know. The Holy Spirit was given to us by God to help us know. We must engage the Spirit by praying in tongues and studying the Word of God to give Him the opportunity to make these things known to our spirits.

> But as it is written: "Eye has not seen, nor ear heard, nor have entered into the heart of man the things which God has prepared for those who love Him." But God has revealed them to us through His Spirit. For the Spirit searches all things, yes, the deep things of God. For what man knows the things of a man except the spirit of the man which is in him? Even so no one knows the things of God except the Spirit of God. Now we have received, not the spirit of the world, but the Spirit who is from God, that we might know the things that have been freely given to us by God.
> —1 Corinthians 2:9-12

The Bible tells us that by knowledge, the rooms are filled with all precious and pleasant riches (Proverb 24:4). We know that God has prepared precious things for those who love Him, but until those who love Him know what has been prepared for them, their rooms, or lives, will remain empty. The Holy Spirit knows every precious thing that God has freely given to us and He wants to reveal them to us, but we must cooperate with Him. There is no better way to do so than to engage Him by praying in the language of the Holy Spirit in man.

Knowledge is strength

Knowledge is strength. The Bible tell us to be strong in the Lord and in the power of his might, and to put on the whole armor of God that we may be able to stand against the wiles of the devil (Ephesians 6:10-11). One of the ways to be strong in the Lord is to grow in our knowledge of Him. There is both head knowledge and heart knowledge of Him. Head knowledge alone leads to bondage, but heart knowledge, which comes from the Holy Spirit's teachings, results in freedom. Spiritual knowledge and understanding give birth to spiritual strength. This is the strength of the faith that overcomes the world (1 John 5:4). Faith comes through knowledge and understanding of God's word.

> A wise man is strong, yes, a man of knowledge increases strength.
>
> —Proverb 24:5

Believers suffer unnecessarily when they do not have knowledge, or when they have the wrong kind of knowledge. Many are still oppressed by the Devil, who, according to the Word of God, is under their feet (Ephesians 1:22; 2:6). Many Christians are afraid of the devil, and testify much about the things he does in their lives. They talk as though they are more afraid of the Devil than they are of God. If you have received the baptism of the Holy Spirit, the One in you is much greater than the Devil (1 John 4:4). Knowledge of the One in you is what gives you strength to resist the Devil until he flees from you in terror (James 4:7). Knowing deep inside your spirit the truth about who you are in Christ and about what Christ has done to the Devil for your sake will free you from oppression. Once you acquire this knowledge and you truly believe it deep in your spirit, you become a threat to the kingdom of darkness. You should not have any fear of him. Your only concern should be the closeness of your relationship with God. "God has not given us a spirit of fear, but of power and of love and of a sound mind" (2 Timothy 1:7). However, if you do not know this, you will live in fear.

> Therefore my people have gone into captivity, because they have no knowledge; their honorable men are famished, and their multitude dried up with thirst.
> —Isaiah 5:13

Where there is no knowledge, even honorable men suffer. Good people can suffer great harm from the Devil, not because God allows it, but because they do not know their rights according to the Scriptures. And when they have been able to stumble on the truth in the Scriptures, they do not have the wisdom to apply it. The Holy Spirit is the spirit of wisdom and understanding (Isaiah 11:2). I believe that if we engage the Spirit as our Helper, praying in tongues frequently, we will be strengthened in our faith and understanding.

> And you shall know the truth, and the truth shall make you free.
> —John 8:32

> But you, beloved, building yourselves up on your most holy faith, praying in the Holy Spirit.
> —Jude 1:20

We cannot know truth unless God reveals it to us. When Peter declared that Jesus was the Christ, Son of the living God, Jesus replied, "Blessed are you, Simon Bar-Jonah, for flesh and blood has not revealed this to you, but My Father who is in heaven" (Matthew 16:17). We cannot know truth in God's Word without the Spirit of God; it has to be given to us supernaturally. As we pray in tongues, these truths are deposited into our spirits by the Holy Spirit. As we call on the name of the Lord with the pure language restored to us, He answers and shows us great and mighty things.

> Call to Me, and I will answer you, and show you great and mighty things, which you do not know.
>
> —Jeremiah 33:3

> For what man knows the things of a man except the spirit of the man which is in him? Even so no one knows the things of God except the Spirit of God. Now we have received, not the spirit of the world, but the Spirit who is from God, that we might know the things that have been freely given to us by God.
>
> —1 Corinthians 2:11-12

The natural world versus the spiritual world

When we become Christians, we are born into a new world where God reigns supreme. There is both a natural world and a supernatural world. Just as natural laws govern our natural world, there are supernatural laws that govern the kingdom of God. Scientists study to unlock the natural laws that govern our natural world to make life better for us on the earth, Christians,

with the Holy Spirit's help, have been given the power and privilege of unlocking the spiritual laws and principles to make life better for mankind in every way. A deep relationship with the Father is the key.

We are natural men, but we have been given the Spirit of God by baptism so we can explore and discover truths in the Word of God to make a difference in our natural world. I believe baptism in the Holy Spirit is our help in this endeavor. Our discoveries in the Word of God, as revealed by the Holy Spirit, can alter our situations in the natural world for the better. Praying in tongues before God will, over time, give the seeker a sense of purpose as God begins to direct the seeker's life either in the secular world or in the ministry. The seeker who spends a lot of time praying in tongues will definitely experience supernatural events more frequently than others. He will have a greater sense of destiny.

The kingdom of darkness versus the kingdom of light

According to the Bible, our natural world is one of darkness, and the kingdom of God is one of light. In the kingdom of darkness, the essentials for true living are hidden. These essentials are revealed to man only by the kingdom of light—God's kingdom. In the kingdom of light, truth reigns. The supernatural world of light has dominion over the natural world. When we discover truth in the Word about the kingdom of God, we can effect changes in our situation by the power of God. God will always respond to the truths we have gleaned from His Word with the help of the Holy Spirit.

Jesus came from the kingdom of light and knew with great intimacy the principles governing it. He was able to suspend the natural laws that govern this world to accomplish the purposes of the kingdom of light. He multiplied five loaves of bread and two fish into enough to feed five thousand men (Matthew 14:13-21). Jesus spoke to the wind and the waves of the sea, and they obeyed his command (Matthew 8:24-27). He turned water into wine (John 2:1-10). In all of these miracles, the laws of nature were suspended to make way for the power of the Spirit of God. Jesus said, "Most assuredly, I say to you, he who believes in Me, the works that I do he will do also; and greater works than these he will do, because I go to My Father" (John 14:12).

Jesus meant what He said. Believers must seek to do the works Jesus did. The Holy Spirit will reveal them to us if we pray and study God's Word. This is how we shine in the world as light. Jesus said, "You are the light of the world. A city that is set on a hill cannot be hidden. Nor do they light a lamp and put it under a basket, but on a lampstand, and it gives light to all who are in the house. Let your light so shine before men, that they may see your good works and glorify your Father in heaven" (Matthew 5:14-16). We need the Holy Spirit's help to discover who we are in Him. Once we discover this, we will lose our fear of the Devil and all that he is able to do to mankind. We will discover that we are in a different class of men. We are the children of God, and we cannot be harassed by the Devil and his angels.

Positioning ourselves

Knowledge of the Holy Spirit's truth helps us position ourselves for showers of blessing from the Lord. Until we place ourselves in the path of God's blessings, we will never be blessed. Understanding the Word of God is what helps us to position ourselves for the blessings of God's exceedingly great and precious promises (2 Peter1:4).

And I should heal them

> And in them the prophecy of Isaiah is fulfilled, which says: "Hearing you will hear and shall not understand, and seeing you will see and not perceive; for the hearts of this people have grown dull. Their ears are hard of hearing, and their eyes they have closed, lest they should see with their eyes and hear with their ears, lest they should understand with their hearts and turn, so that I should heal them."
>
> —Matthew 13:14-15

The seeing and hearing mentioned in this passage are not the kind done with our physical eyes and ears. The Bible is speaking of our spiritual eyes and ears, which must receive instruction from the Word of God through the power of the Holy Spirit. Once the eyes and ears are opened to the truth, spiritual understanding follows. This takes place in the heart, where faith is born. Faith in the heart helps the believer to turn, or position himself for a miracle or answer from God. Jesus said that once a person turns, He should heal him (Matthew 13:15).

Many Christians know the Word of God and the promises of the Scriptures, but they do not have enough understanding from the Holy Spirit to make the proper turn to receive the blessings. Spiritual understanding of the Word of God is what leads to the faith that receives the promise. Jude tells us that praying in the spirit will help strengthen our faith in God (Jude 1:20). This means that praying in tongues will help us understand the word of God in the core of our being: our hearts. Praying in the Holy Spirit, therefore, will help us turn so that He can heal us, or give us our desired answer.

When we receive the Holy Spirit, we are given access to the deep truths of God. We can enter into a lifetime of discovery in the kingdom of God with the help of the Holy Spirit. The Holy Spirit is the only One on the earth today who knows the truths and secrets of God (1 Corinthians 2:10). He, like Jesus, wants to share these things with us so we can receive the full benefit of all Jesus purchased for us on the cross.

The glory of secrets

The Bible suggests that God takes delight in keeping secrets. These secrets, when discovered or unveiled, are always of great benefit to mankind. However, the secrets are never revealed without a serious search for them.

> It is the glory of God to conceal a matter, but the glory of kings is to search out a matter.
>
> —Proverb 25:2

> The secret things belong to the Lord our God, but those things which are revealed belong to us and to our children forever, that we may do all the words of this law.
>
> —Deuteronomy 29:29

Language from Heaven

God receives glory for concealing a matter, but the glory of kings is to search the matter out. The Bible tells us that God has made us kings and priests in the kingdom of God (Revelation 1:6). If we want our lives to be made beautiful, if we want God to be glorified in our lives, we must search out these secrets. He came to console those who mourned in Zion, "to give them beauty for ashes, the oil of joy for mourning, the garment of praise for the spirit of heaviness" (Isaiah 61:3). The Holy Spirit is given to us for a search that cannot fail, but we have to engage the Spirit in our search. Again, the only way to do so is to study the word of God and pray in tongues.

Everything that is precious in life requires work to obtain. Gold, silver, diamonds, and petroleum are not found on the surface of the earth; you have to dig deep to find them. This is the way God wants it. If you want to find, you must seek. If you want to receive, you must ask. If you want the door to be opened for you, you must knock (Matthew 7:7). There is no way around these principles. You must have a desire to know the things that God wants to reveal. In addition to that desire, you must search. Deep calls out to deep (Psalm 42:7). If you need more of God, you must hunger and thirst for more of God. This will put you in a search mode. As you ask, seek, and knock, you shall receive from the Lord.

> Ask, and it will be given to you; seek, and you will find; knock, and it will be opened to you. For everyone who asks receives, and he who seeks finds, and to him who knocks it will be opened.
>
> —Matthew 7:7-8

It seems God will allow an important matter to lie fallow until the believer has enough desire in Him to ask about it. There is nothing too big or too great to ask God for. Moses asked to see God's glory. God granted his desire (Exodus 33:18-22). Hezekiah the king was sick, so the Lord sent Isaiah the prophet to tell him to put his house in order because death was near. Hezekiah prayed and wept before God, and was heard. God sent the prophet Isaiah to him again to tell him that his prayers had been heard, and that God would add fifteen more years to his life (Isaiah 38:1-8). It is certain, then, that if we ask, we will receive, if we seek, we will find, and if we knock, the door will be opened to us. The assurance of an answer to our prayers from God is even much greater in the New Testament because we have a Mediator of a better covenant established on better promises (Hebrews 8:6). Moreover, we have the Holy Spirit in our lives through the Spirit's baptism. He helps us with our prayer lives as we pray in the spirit with our pure language from heaven.

What the Bible says about the believer

Nicodemus, a ruler of the Jews, came to Jesus by night to enquire about the kingdom of God, as he had no doubt that Jesus was truly a man of God. Jesus talked to him about the born-again experience, which baffled Nicodemus. He saw what Jesus was saying from the natural viewpoint, but Jesus was talking about spiritual birth. In one of Jesus' statements to Nicodemus, he made a statement which I consider a description of what the born-again believer is:

> That which is born of the flesh is flesh, and that which is
> born of the Spirit is spirit. Do not marvel that I said to
> you, "You must be born again." The wind blows where

Language from Heaven

it wishes, and you hear the sound of it, but cannot tell where it comes from and where it goes. So is everyone who is born of the Spirit.

—John 3:7-8

In the above statement, Jesus was not describing the wind or the Spirit, but the born-again believer. This is how he characterized the believer: He is like the wind. He is flesh, but He is also born of the Spirit of God. His spirit, therefore, has the nature of God in it. God wants us to share His divine nature (2 Peter 1:4).

Jesus also spoke of the believer as the light of the world (Matthew 5:14). We are used to singing songs like, "This little light of mine, I am going to let it shine." But Jesus did not come to give us only a "little light." He called us the light of the world! A little light will not light up the world. I believe we who are born of the Spirit embrace less rather than drawing from the Holy Spirit the things God has freely given. The reason for this is because the Holy Spirit has not been given His rightful place in the church. Jesus said that when the Holy Spirit comes, He will guide us into truth (John 16:13). Receiving the Holy Spirit with the ability to pray in tongues is the first step to being able to unlock the mysteries of the kingdom of God for our benefit. Knowing the mysteries of the kingdom is what changes our lives. The Holy Spirit is the only one who can make that happen.

Signs and wonders

The prophet Isaiah spoke of Jesus and His church, talking about what they would be like in the last days.

> Here am I and the children whom the Lord has given me! We are for signs and wonders in Israel from the Lord of hosts, Who dwells in Mount Zion.
>
> —Isaiah 8:18

Believers are for signs and wonders from the Lord of hosts. God spoke of all believers, not just some privileged ones. We are the light of the world! We are the salt of the earth! We are a mystery on the earth. No wonder we are misunderstood by the natural people of the world. No wonder we are misjudged by those who do not know Him. The statement above by Isaiah the prophet agrees with the words of Jesus:

> And these signs will follow those who believe: In My name they will cast out demons; they will speak with new tongues;they will take up serpents; and if they drink anything deadly, it will by no means hurt them; they will lay hands on the sick, and they will recover.
>
> —Mark 16:17-18

We are given signs and wonders by God. It behooves the believer to search for and obtain all that God has given. With the help of the Holy Spirit, we can rise to the level of believers in the early church doing signs and wonders in the name of the Lord. The Holy Spirit's baptism will bring us to that place; it is the doorway to the realm of miracles and wonders. Praying in the Spirit will bring all believers there. Accepting the supernatural will prevent men from accepting man's philosophies about creation and life. Signs and wonders convince the skeptic of God, although some may still refuse to believe because they love darkness rather than light (John 3:19). In biblical times, many believed when they saw the miracles that Jesus performed, and many today will believe when they see the miracles that He is performing through believers.

Jesus' will is for the believer to be able to do the same miracles that He did in His earthly ministry, and more.

> Most assuredly, I say to you, he who believes in Me, the works that I do he will do also; and greater works than these he will do, because I go to My Father.
>
> —John 14:12

The above passage is surprising, considering all the wonders Jesus did, but He assured us that the believer is equipped to do the same. Why do we not see these miracles performed by believers today? Jesus is the same yesterday, today, and forever (Hebrews 13:8). What has changed? The church must be willing to embrace the supernatural. The church must give the Holy Spirit His rightful place in our life. We must rely on Him and pray through Him to be enlightened and emboldened to do the same works as Jesus for the world to see and be amazed by. If we cannot accept praying in tongues, which is the first step into the workings of the Holy Spirit, how can we accept and receive the miracles and wonders Jesus spoke of?

> Praying always with all prayer and supplication in the Spirit, being watchful to this end with all perseverance and supplication for all the saints—and for me, that utterance may be given to me, that I may open my mouth boldly to make known the mystery of the gospel.
>
> —Ephesians 6:18-19

To pray in the Spirit, we must pray in tongues. When believers in the Christian world do this, utterance will be given to the ministers of the gospel, and they will be able to open their mouths boldly to reveal the mysteries of the gospel, resulting in signs and wonders as it did with Peter, Paul, Steven, and Philip the evangelist.

The Scripture above encourages the believer to pray always. For Christians, praying must be a lifestyle. Also, according to Paul, prayer must be in the Spirit (Ephesians 6:18). Paul said that all prayer and supplication must be in the Spirit. As we pray in this way for all believers, including ministers of the gospel, boldness will be given to all who preach the gospel. I am sure God will confirm His Word with signs (Mark 16:20).

God's special people

Believers are "a chosen generation, a royal priesthood, a holy nation, God's own special people, called to proclaim the praises of Him who called them out of darkness into His marvelous light (1 Peter 2:9). Every born-again Christian is royalty; we belong to the royal priesthood. Every born-again person is special. We are a holy nation, and our lives and works should proclaim the praises of God. If this is the case, why then are so many born-again children of God fearful, uncertain about life, and unknowledgeable about the supernatural even though they have been supernaturally born into the family of God? The reason is that many have not fully embraced the Holy Spirit as the head of the church in the physical absence of our Lord Jesus Christ. They have accepted Him, but not the way the first-century church did.

There is fear in the camp, and this fear has prevented many from receiving the baptism in the Holy Spirit with tongues. Some are afraid of the supernatural. Why should a Christian be afraid of something that is clearly spoken of in the Bible? God is a good Father who cares deeply for all who have accepted Christ as Lord and Savior. God would not offer anything that would hurt the believer. What He offers will make life beautiful for the believer, spiritually and in the natural world. God is a great Father!

There should be no fear in the heart of Christians. Natural fears are helpful for making us cautious of dangers and hurtful things. However, fears that paralyze us, preventing us from living life to the fullest, are not of God. The Bible tells us that God has not given us the spirit of fear, but of power, of love, and of a sound mind. Through the Holy Spirit, we have all the power we need to do what God has given to us to do. Through the power of the Holy Spirit, we can truly love—we can even love our enemies.

Through the power of the Holy Spirit, our minds are sound. Christ has become for us the wisdom of God (1 Corinthians 1:30). We have the mind of Christ (1 Corinthians 2:16), and Christ's mind is not subject to depression. Christ's mind is not subject to confusion or despair. There is always hope in Christ. These things have been delivered to us through the Holy Spirit. We did receive the Spirit of power, of love, and of a sound mind. Praying in tongues constantly will deliver these blessings into our life.

When the Holy Spirit came into the world on the day of Pentecost, speaking in tongues was a clear sign of His coming. Praying in tongues was His gift for all to call on the name of the Lord. If this gift is not stirred up; if this gift is not actively engaged frequently with lengthy sessions, the believer is left with nothing but to lean on his own understanding. This will leave the believer spiritually weak, struggling to gain understanding without the help of the Spirit of God.

The Bible tells us that God gave all who received him the right to become children of God (John 1:12). As children of God, we should have some of the attributes of the Savior, who is the only begotten Son of the Father. God wants us to be more like Jesus in every way. Jesus was the Master. The Bible tells us, "Here am I and the children whom the Lord has given to Me! We are for signs and wonders" (Isaiah 8:18).

Every believer belongs to God's royal priesthood. Priests are a special group of people who have the privilege of standing in the presence of God. Our place in and power over the events that take place on earth cannot be overemphasized. God has placed an awesome responsibility on us as believers. However, everywhere we look we see believers who seem to be struggling just to survive. Jesus said:

> You are the salt of the earth; but if the salt loses its flavor, how shall it be seasoned? It is then good for nothing but to be thrown out and trampled underfoot by men. You are the light of the world. A city that is set on a hill cannot be hidden. Nor do they light a lamp and put it under a basket, but on a lampstand, and it gives light to all who are in the house. Let your light so shine before men, that they may see your good works and glorify your Father in heaven.
>
> —Matthew 5:13-16

The believer is the salt of the earth and the light of the world. The world would be in darkness without believers. The world will be tasteless without the presence of believers. Why is this? Doubtless, it is the presence of the Holy Spirit in the lives of believers. The Holy Spirit has been sent to the earth to accomplish a mission,

LANGUAGE FROM HEAVEN

and His vehicle of choice is the body of the one who has been made clean by the blood of the Son of God. The believer must cooperate with the Holy Spirit to accomplish this work. The believer must take on the Holy Spirit's mission as his own and engage the Holy Spirit's power.

God has given the believer much authority on the earth, but many believers are still not aware of what they have been given. Jesus said:

> Assuredly, I say to you, whatever you bind on earth will
> be bound in heaven, and whatever you loose on earth
> will be loosed in heaven.
>
> —Matthew 18:18

Through prayer and fasting believers can change natural events on the earth to benefit the kingdom of God, but they have to desire the change and then engage the power of the Scriptures and the Holy Spirit. I believe that Christians could turn economies and events in the world around if they would engage the power that God has given to them. We can try to make changes through political means, but lasting change only comes when believers engage the power of the Holy Spirit to change things for the better.

> If My people who are called by My name will humble
> themselves, and pray and seek My face, and turn from
> their wicked ways, then I will hear from heaven, and
> will forgive their sin and heal their land.
>
> —2 Chronicles 7:14

CHAPTER 13

BETTER FOR YOU THAT
I GO AWAY

Before Jesus went to the cross to die for the sins of the world, he gathered the disciples to unveil a number of incredible truths about Himself, the Father God, the Holy Spirit, the disciples, and their mission for God (John chapters 13-17). He also taught them the new kind of love: a new commandment to love one another as Jesus had loved them. He told them that by their love for one another, men would recognize them as true disciples of Jesus (John 13:34-35). This kind of love is not found on the earth; it came from heaven. It is present in every believer's heart because of the presence of the Holy Spirit in the believer's life.

Jesus told the disciples that He was leaving the world, that He came from the Father, and that he was going back to the Father. It was clear to the disciples that once Jesus left the earth to be with His Father, they would no longer be able to see, touch, or hear Him. Sorrow filled their hearts. To comfort them, Jesus said, "Nevertheless I tell you the truth, it is to your advantage that

I go away; for if I do not go away, the Helper will not come to you; but if I depart, I will send Him to you" (John 16:7). Jesus told the disciples that they would be better off in life if He left them, because the Holy Spirit would then be sent to them and all believers forever.

> And I will pray the Father, and He will give you another Helper, that He may abide with you forever—the Spirit of truth, Whom the world cannot receive, because it neither sees Him nor knows Him; but you know Him, for He dwells with you and will be in you.
>
> —John 14:16-17

If you ask any reasonable man whom he would rather have with him all the time—Jesus or the Holy Spirit—he would probably choose Jesus. However, God, who created us and knows all things, says it is to our advantage to have the Helper with us all the time instead of Jesus in human form. Jesus would be working from the outside in, but the Holy Spirit works from the inside out. This is a better deal for every child of God, but because many have not renewed their minds according to verses 1 and 2 in Romans 12, they still think it would be better to have Jesus in human flesh than the Holy Spirit in all His glory and power.

The fact that Jesus said we would be better off when the Holy Spirit had come to live with us underscores the importance of the Holy Spirit in the believer's life. The Christian life is life with the Holy Spirit. As many as are led by the Spirit of God, these are the children of God (Romans 8:14).

Having the Holy Spirit is the only way we are able to be like the Son of God in this world. We will not be able to do the works that

Jesus did on the earth without the Holy Spirit inside us. The Holy Spirit was fully in Jesus, and with His anointing, Jesus changed the world. He offered Himself through the eternal Spirit (Acts 10:38, Hebrews 9:14). The Holy Spirit truly is the Helper! We need help in every area of life, and the Holy Spirit will help us if we let Him. In our spiritual lives, we need the Helper. In our relationships with one another, within the family or without, we need Him. We need Him involved in our marriages and our finances. We need Him in order to stay healthy and physically strong. He is the life-giving Spirit. The more of Him we have in our lives, the better our lives will be. The greater the anointing of the Holy Spirit we have in our life, the greater our power over the issues of life.

The evidence of Jesus's words in Peter

Peter and the other disciples seemed confused about the mysteries of the kingdom of God before Jesus went to the cross to die for our sins. The apostle Peter denied knowing Jesus three times before the Savior's death, but after the resurrection, and especially after he received the baptism of the Holy Spirit, Peter was a changed man. The other disciples were changed also. Peter had preached the gospel before the day of Pentecost, but God did not see it fit to record his message in the Bible (Luke 9:1-2). Peter's message to all who had gathered in Jerusalem for the feast of Pentecost was a masterpiece. He was so eloquent, and the power of the Holy Spirit in him was so strong, that three thousand people turned their lives over to the Lord Jesus (Acts 2:14-42). The Holy Spirit recorded this message in the Bible.

One very important thing Peter said on the day of Pentecost was "Repent, and let every one of you be baptized in the name of

Jesus Christ for the remission of sins; and you shall receive the gift of the Holy Spirit. For the promise is to you, and to your children, and to all who are afar off, as many as the Lord our God will call" (Acts 2:38-39). Receiving the Holy Spirit is portrayed as a promise from God to everyone who believes. God never forgets his promise, and is always ready to make good on his promises. The Holy Spirit is for everyone called by God to become a Christian. They can receive the promise of the Holy Spirit as soon as they have answered his call to become believers. Every believer will receive in the same way Peter and the other disciples did, with speaking in tongues the primary evidence of the Holy Spirit's presence in the believer.

Miracles and signs

Jesus said those who believe in Him would perform the miracles He did (John 14:12). His words were fulfilled in the lives of the believers after they received the Holy Spirit. The disciples received the Holy Spirit and spoke in tongues at the beginning of Acts chapter 2. In Acts 5:12, many miracles were done among the people by the apostles', and there was great unity among those who believed. Steven was chosen with six others to serve tables. He was full of the Holy Ghost, faith, and wisdom (Acts 6:3-5).

> And Stephen, full of faith and power, did great wonders
> and signs among the people.
>
> —Acts 6:8

Jesus and the children whom the Lord has given to Him serve as signs and wonders (Isaiah 8:18). After the Holy Ghost came, that Scripture became a living reality in the lives of the disciples of Jesus Christ. So many supernatural things were taking place in the lives of the disciples that the new believers were a threat to the political powers. Phillip went down to the city of Samaria and preached Christ to the people. They listened to what he had to say and believed because of the miracles he performed in the name of Jesus (Acts 8:6). This was the power of the Holy Spirit at work. Thank God that the disciples in the early church made sure that everyone who believed received the baptism of the Holy Spirit to empower them to be true witnesses of the resurrection of the Lord Jesus Christ.

> And it happened, while Apollos was at Corinth, that Paul, having passed through the upper regions, came to Ephesus. And finding some disciples he said to them, "Did you receive the Holy Spirit when you believed?"
> —Acts 19:1-2

> But you shall receive power when the Holy Spirit has come upon you; and you shall be witnesses to Me in Jerusalem, and in all Judea and Samaria, and to the end of the earth.
> —Acts 1:8

The power the disciples had to do miracles and wonders in the name of Jesus Christ was the power Jesus spoke of in Acts 1:8. They received the power when they were filled with the Holy Spirit, and they could preach the gospel in the same way Jesus had, with miracles. Jesus had said, "He who believes in Me, the works that I do he will do also; and greater works than these he will do, because I go to My Father" (John 14:12). His words were fulfilled in the ministry of the disciples, and His words are still being fulfilled today in the lives of those who wholeheartedly accept what the Bible says about the Holy Spirit, and His ability to make the believer a powerful witness for Christ. Jesus has gone to be with the Father, and now believers are doing the same works that He did.

Peter's shadow and Paul's handkerchiefs

There is an interesting account about the disciples in the book of Acts that is similar to the ministry of Jesus while He was on the earth.

> And believers were increasingly added to the Lord, multitudes of both men and women, so that they brought the sick out into the streets and laid them on beds and couches, that at least the shadow of Peter passing by might fall on some of them. Also a multitude gathered from the surrounding cities to Jerusalem, bringing sick people and those who were tormented by unclean spirits, and they were all healed.
>
> —Acts 5:14-16

The Peter we read about in the above passage is different from the Peter of the gospels. He was the same man, but a different person. He was so full of the Holy Spirit after the day of Pentecost that everyone recognized the authority and power at work in his life. Peter's shadow healed the sick as he passed by! We do not read anywhere in the gospels that Jesus' shadow healed the sick, but Peter's did. The words of Jesus were fulfilled in his life (John

14:12). People were brought from surrounding cities to the church for healing, and all were healed. Jesus is the same yesterday, today, and forever (Hebrews 13:8). What has happened to the church? Have the leaders of the modern church denied the power of the Holy Spirit, or do people no longer truly believe what the Bible says, instead acknowledging that the Bible speaks of these things, but they may not be relevant in our time? This type of reasoning and belief will render the church powerless and ineffective in the making of true disciple.

Paul also performed special miracles in his ministry to the Gentiles.

> Now God worked unusual miracles by the hands of Paul, so that even handkerchiefs or aprons were brought from his body to the sick, and the diseases left them and the evil spirits went out of them.
>
> —Acts 19:11-12

Handkerchiefs from Paul's body made the sick and diseased well. The handkerchiefs cast out demons from people! What was in those handkerchiefs? I believe the power of the One who cannot be confined to a specific location; it was the power of the Holy Spirit in Paul's life. Paul's physical presence was not significant. It was the Lord's doing and it is marvelous in our eyes.

Based on the experiences of the disciples in the early church, it does seem that it was best for them that Jesus left to be with the Father. He said the Helper would not come if He stayed on the earth (John 16:7). If Jesus had stayed on the earth, the disciples would have depended on Him for all things, but in His absence and with the help and guidance of the Holy Spirit, they changed the world. We could do the same today if we rely on the power of the Holy Spirit. This is the power that is at work inside us (Ephesians 3:20).

The Holy Spirit was in charge in the early church

The disciples of the early church heard, believed, and lived by the words of Jesus. No wonder they were so powerful! They knew that the Holy Spirit was the One to take the place of Jesus in their lives and they allowed Him to fill them up in baptism. They spoke with tongues and the Holy Spirit gave utterance, and they listened to His instructions when He spoke.

> As they ministered to the Lord and fasted, the Holy Spirit said, "Now Separate to Me Barnabas and Saul for the work to which I have called them." Then, having fasted and prayed, and laid hands on them, they sent them away. So, being sent out by the Holy Spirit, they went down to Seleucia, and from there they sailed to Cyprus.
>
> —Acts 13:2-4

At the church at Antioch, certain prophets and teachers, including Paul and Barnabas, were having a prayer meeting when the Holy Spirit spoke, asking the church at Antioch to separate Barnabas and Paul to the Holy Spirit for the work He had called them to. The Holy Spirit was the One doing the calling. He is the Lord of the harvest. He is the One in charge. Jesus did not call Barnabas and Paul; the Holy Spirit did. Jesus is seated at the Father's right hand in heaven, but the Holy Spirit is the One in charge of the work of the Godhead on earth. The church did not send them out; the Holy Spirit did. We are in the dispensation of the Holy Spirit. Every believer must make room for the Holy Spirit in his or her life, or else the Christian walk will not be as God has planned it. The key to the Christian life is the leadership and help of the Holy Spirit. The Holy Spirit cannot help those who do not pay close attention to the words of Jesus and what He said about the Holy Spirit.

> For as many as are led by the Spirit of God, these are
> sons of God.
>
> —Romans 8:14

The Holy Spirit chooses who is sent, to where, and what they must do. He is the Lord of the harvest. We are living in harvest time, and we cannot truly partake in divine harvest without the power of the Holy Spirit. Paul and Barnabas' missionary journeys began with the call of the Holy Spirit. He sent them out and worked through them to accomplish His purpose.

The Holy Spirit directs what is and is not accepted in the practice of Christianity. This is the way it was in the early church. The Holy Spirit decides. The will of the Holy Spirit has been put down in writing in the Bible. The Bible tells us that "all Scripture is given by inspiration of God, and is profitable for doctrine, for reproof, for correction, for instruction in righteousness, that the man of God may be complete, thoroughly equipped for every good work" (2 Timothy 3:16-17). Peter wrote, "For prophecy never came by the will of man, but holy men of God spoke as they were moved by the Holy Spirit" (2 Peter 1:21).

In the New Testament days as recorded in the book of Acts, the Holy Spirit was the One who the disciples turned to when they had disagreements about what was acceptable regarding the practice of

LANGUAGE FROM HEAVEN

Christianity. After Paul and Barnabas had completed their first missionary journey, they returned to Antioch. Certain disciples from Judea joined them. They, however, were not sent by the elders and apostles in Jerusalem. These disciples began to say that the Gentile Christians must be circumcised according to the Law of Moses before they could be saved. Paul and Barnabas disagreed with them. There was a great dispute, and Paul and Barnabas were sent to ask the elders and apostles in Jerusalem for answers.

There was a dispute in the council at Jerusalem as well, but the matter concluded when the elders and apostles discovered what the Holy Spirit wanted for the church. They sent a letter to the Gentile church:

> It seemed good to the Holy Spirit, and to us, to lay upon you no greater burden than these necessary things: that you abstain from things offered to idols, from blood, from things strangled, and from sexual immorality. If you keep yourselves from these, you will do well. Farewell.
>
> —Acts 15:28-29

The Holy Spirit worked with the disciples in the early church, empowering them, teaching them, and directing their activities. We can now fully understand what Jesus meant when He said:

> But because I have said these things to you, sorrow has filled your heart. Nevertheless I tell you the truth. It is to your advantage that I go away; for if I do not go away, the Helper will not come to you; but if I depart, I will send Him to you.
>
> —John 16:6-7

It is hard to understand how one can live as a Christian without the help of the Holy Spirit. Jesus, our Lord and Savior, loved us so much that He gave His life to save us, but for our own good, He decided it would be better for us if he left to be with the Father. His departure is what cleared the way for the Holy Spirit to come to us. God has so much in store for every believer, but we cannot obtain any of it without the help of the Holy Spirit, who will abide with us forever (John 14:16). The least a Christian can do is to welcome the Holy Spirit by allowing Him to come into his or her life in baptism.

The two classes of believers

The Scriptures discuss two stages of growth in the Christian walk. The belief systems of the church today regarding the presence of the Holy Spirit in the believer's life seem to yield two different classes of believers: those who have the Holy Spirit with them, and those who have the Holy Spirit in them ("Spirit-filled" believers).

> And I will pray the Father, and He will give you another Helper, that He may abide with you forever—the Spirit of truth, whom the world cannot receive, because it neither sees Him nor knows Him; but you know Him, for He dwells with you and will be in you.
> —John 14: 16-17

God did not intend for there to be two groups of believers in the church. Every believer should be filled with the Holy Spirit. Jesus told the disciples that by being with Him, they had come to know the person of the Holy Spirit. He said that the Spirit was

 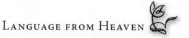

dwelling with them at that time, but eventually He would be in them—he was speaking of the day of Pentecost when the disciples would receive the baptism of the Holy Spirit and speak in tongues. All who receive Christ have the Holy Spirit dwelling with them through life, but when they receive the Holy Spirit, He then lives in them. Inside the believer, He is better able to instruct and teach the ways of the Lord. This is why the apostles were so keen on every new believer receiving the baptism of the Holy Spirit.

> And it happened, while Apollos was at Corinth, that Paul, having passed through the upper regions, came to Ephesus. And finding some disciples he said to them, "Did you receive the Holy Spirit when you believed?"
> —Acts 19:1-2

CHAPTER 14

My Journey

In the Old Testament, the Holy Spirit spoke through the prophet Isaiah about Jesus and the New Testament believers:

> Here am I and the children whom the Lord has given me! We are for signs and wonders in Israel from the Lord of hosts, Who dwells in Mount Zion.
>
> —Isaiah 8:18

The above passage clearly refers to Jesus and believers of the New Testament era. We are signs and wonders from the Lord of hosts to the world. In my life as a new Christian, Scriptures like the one above gave me much trouble. I knew very few Christians then who could claim to be part of this passage in Isaiah, but most Christians I knew could not be part of the group Isaiah spoke about. Reading the words of Jesus in the gospel according to John further complicated the matter for me:

Language from Heaven

Most assuredly, I say to you, he who believes in Me, the works that I do he will do also; and greater works than these he will do, because I go to My Father.

—John 14:12

I wondered if I was a true believer, and if I was, why were there no signs or wonders in my service as a Christian? All around me were powerless, fearful Christians wondering whether their relationships with Jesus were okay, and looking to just a tiny group of fellow believers for answers. There was even a time in my early days as a Christian when I asked out loud what it would take to free myself from the feeling that I was not truly saved. The answer I was given was that we walk by faith and not by sight (2 Corinthians 5:7). The answers I was given did not make sense to me then because I had not been properly taught, and I was certainly not looking to the Holy Spirit for answers. I noticed that many around me were also struggling with the things of God. Some of the people we considered to be leaders appeared, to my mind, not to walk with the confidence I would expect from those who truly knew the Master. I wanted to see the confidence I had read about in the book of Acts.

Therefore my people have gone into captivity, because they have no knowledge; their honorable men are famished, and their multitude dried up with thirst.

—Isaiah 5:13

These things were heavy on my mind in the early 1980s. I wondered why things were the way they were. I began to study the Scriptures and to question some of my own beliefs. I was filled with the Holy Spirit a month or so after I received Christ as Lord and Savior. I spoke in tongues for a while (not consistently), but then I stopped doing so as doubt grew in my heart.

Visits with witch doctors

I received Christ in 1975 as my Lord and Savior, but early in 1980, although I was following the ways of the Christian faith and living the best Christian life I knew how to, my life was filled with uncertainties, insecurities, and fears. I knew I was under great oppression from the enemy because of the way I had lived my life as a child and as a young man before I accepted Christ as Savior.

When I was a child, I was very sickly, according to my mother. She believed I had been bewitched through a witch doctor by someone in her extended family. Back then she believed the situation was beyond remedy by western medicine, so she considered visits to witch doctors the only possible solution. This was before the power of Jesus Christ became a powerful force in Nigeria.

These visits involved what I consider worship services to the demons behind the witch doctors' powers. There were animal sacrifices, and then feasts of meat from the animals slaughtered for these gods. I did not understand what the adults were doing during these sacrifices, but I did enjoy the meat! I never liked praying to the idols they made us pray to. I thought they looked ugly! Most of them were carved wood in the shape of men. Some had crooked noses with mouths where they would not normally be on a human face. I could not understand why the adults thought that a lifeless thing like that could protect us from the troubles of life.

LANGUAGE FROM HEAVEN

Fear reigned

As I grew older, I began to understand why the adults in my life did what they did. Evil was real, and demons did exist. There was fear everywhere. Demons were having a field day in the lives of most people because there was little knowledge of the power of the gospel of Jesus Christ. We were particularly afraid of witches and those with familiar spirits. I began to visit witch doctors on my own when I was about twenty years old, just for protection from witches. Many around me were also afraid, and the witch doctors made us feel that only they possessed powers of protection. I had no idea that I was fellowshipping with demons.

What I do know now is that anyone who goes to a witch doctor, a palm reader, a psychic, or even plays with anything that has to do with the occult is likely to contract a demon or two. They will make life very painful for you. That is what happened to me. After I received Christ as Savior, by God's mercy, the presence of demons in my life because of my activities with witch doctors in the past surfaced, and I had to deal with it. I did not know before I was saved that demons truly existed, but as I endeavored to draw closer to God, I suddenly became aware of the reality of their existence. I began to feel movements within my body that I could not explain. Something moved all over my body, especially in my chest. I was confused! Today, the church would say that I was in need of deliverance.

I came to the conclusion that there was a demonic presence in my life. As a Christian, I felt fear and confusion. Many seasoned believers concurred, but they had very little knowledge of how I could be helped. My initial understanding when I was first saved was that any demons would disappear when I received Christ as Lord and Savior. Sadly, I discovered that that was not the case.

A minister who took interest in my well-being tried to help a number of times, but could not explain to my satisfaction why I was experiencing demonic oppressions as a Christian. I believe my problems would have been more manageable if I had had good teachers to help me. I sought God's help, and in His mercy, He showed me how to be free from oppression.

The days I lived as a Christian oppressed by demonic forces from my past were a low point in my life. During this time, it was hard to trust God for anything. Praying in tongues was hard to do because it caused the strange movements in my body to increase, and that scared me. So I stopped praying in tongues, but this did not make things better for me spiritually.

Fasting with prayer

In 1982, my hunger for God grew. I could not go back to the world because of the enemy's oppression. Going to hell was not an option for me. I knew that I would be standing before God one day in judgment, and I did not want be fearful when I saw Him face to face. The only place to run was to the throne of God. I wanted answers, and since I was not getting them from men, I went to God. I believed in the Bible. I thought, He is a good God, and will not turn me away. He would hear me if I obeyed His word and fasted and prayed for answers. I had received a lot of good teaching about fasting and prayer, and I wanted to put this truth to the test. If it worked, I would obtain my freedom, and my life would be different. Thank God I made that decision. God helped me greatly. He is such a good and faithful Father. His love has no bounds, and His mercy endures forever!

Seven days of fasting in a hotel room

The desire to seek God with a fast came to me as a student at The University of Georgia. I had to wait until the end of the quarter to carry out my plan. As soon as the quarter was over, I went to a nearby town and rented a hotel room for seven days. I had some helpful books that dealt with the subject of my concern. I also took my Bible with me. I sought the Lord in that little hotel room. God was gracious! I had read from the Scriptures that every believer, in the name of Jesus, has authority from the Lord to cast out devils. I was not only a believer, but it was my own body, my life that was being oppressed. I believed I had the right in God to determine who influenced the way my body felt. I spoke to the demonic influences and commanded them to leave. The movements in my body and other manifestations increased, but I knew I was getting closer to freedom. I coughed violently each time I addressed those demonic forces. I lost my fear of demons, especially those oppressing my life. They left and I became a free man in Christ, ready to explore the Scriptures for all the benefits Christ on the cross left for me in this present world and the one to come.

It was during this period of fasting that I became keenly aware of some of the benefits of praying in tongues. I knew God gave tongues to us for a reason and I made up my mind that as long as I lived, I would never again cease from praying in tongues for any reason. I made a decision to spend a few minutes daily praying in tongues. If what I considered demonic movements increased in my body because I prayed in tongues, so be it. However, I believed that they would cease because I had found my way to true freedom in Christ. My resolve to pray in tongues frequently and for lengthy periods of time was solid. This was possibly the best decision I have ever made in my entire Christian life, except for the decision to accept Christ as my Lord and Savior. The result was instantaneous. My understanding and confidence in God grew tremendously. Little did I know that my stay in that little hotel room for those seven days would completely change my walk with God, leading to the saving of a number of souls, with many receiving the baptism of the Holy Spirit and finding their freedom in Christ!

The beginning of insight and boldness

When I left that hotel room after the period of fasting, my body ached. I felt like I had been in a serious fight and received blow after blow. Someone asked me if God had spoken to me. My answer was in the negative. I had not heard God's voice, but I knew something in me was different. When the aches ceased, a feeling of joy and peace came over me. I began to study the Scriptures again with joy in my heart. I could understand the Scriptures and tie truths from different parts of the Bible together without a teacher's help. It was exciting! I was faithful to my decision to spend time praying daily in tongues. I felt like I needed to catch up since I had wasted much time during the period of my oppression.

The demonic oppressions became a thing of the past, except for occasional frightening incidents at night. When these occurred, I would feel a dark shadow over me, and I would be suddenly conscious of what was happening, but unable to move or speak. I would attempt to call on the name of Jesus for deliverance, but could not even speak His name out loud. Each of these incidents only lasted a short time, but felt like an eternity! I knew they were from the Devil. Someone had told me back in my native country

that they were a bad thing that could culminate in a physical manifestation of something in my body like a terminal disease. I do not know how true that is, but I wanted these occasional incidents to stop.

The oppressions during sleep ceased

Despite the occasional oppressions I was still determined to continue acting on the truth I had gleaned from God's Word that there is great benefit to praying in the Spirit. I was sure that praying in tongues consistently and for long periods of time would change my Christian life. However, I was getting frustrated by the constant attacks from the enemy: the shadows that came over me in my sleep to totally immobilize me from time to time. I cried to God after each episode, calling to Jesus and pleading the blood of Jesus, but the oppressions did not cease.

One night, it happened once again, and in desperation, I cried out again to God for help, asking why. Then a voice spoke to me gently, rebuking me for the way I had been handling the situation. He said, "Why are you crying to me? The little demon who did that to you while you slept is still there in your room, laughing at you because you are reacting fearfully to his oppression." Suddenly my eyes were opened! I knew it was just a little demon doing this to me, and I had allowed it to continue because I did not take authority over the demon in the name of Jesus. I immediately commanded the demon to stand right in front of me. I saw nothing, but believed he was doing exactly what I had commanded him to do in the name of Jesus. Jesus gave me that authority. Then I spoke to the demon, letting him know that I knew my place in Christ, and that he had no authority to oppress me in that way. Then I commanded the demon to leave. After this encounter, I had great peace. It was a lesson in the power of God in a believer's life. The oppression ceased!

You should be speaking more

I experienced a noticeable sign that God had begun to unveil His word to me. Often, I shared some of the things I assumed every Christian knew with one of my Christian schoolmates. From time to time, she appeared shocked by the truths I was sharing from the Scriptures. She would ask, "Where did you get that from?" or "Who taught you that?" Surprised, I would reply, "I thought everyone knew these things." She asked that I speak more about what I was sharing with her with other believers in our Christian group on campus. I took her advice and began to speak more. I began to speak with newfound boldness and confidence that God was giving me as I prayed even more in tongues. I began to be unafraid of people's opinions and thoughts about what I believed and did in Christ. Whether or not they got offended by what I was sharing was not a significant issue as long as I could support my position with the Scriptures. God was faithful in confirming to the others what He was showing me. I received much comfort from His presence and work in my life!

Another factor in the change that God was bringing to my life was the fact that more and more people listened and responded positively to what I had to share. Christianity was becoming more exciting for me. It became more than just a religion, more than going to church—it became my life.

 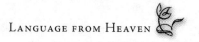

First encounter with a demonic spirit

It was 1980, and I was trying very hard to protect the life of one of the converts God had given to me in my first few years in the USA. This convert was going through a tough time receiving victory over a situation she found herself in. My solution to her problem was to tell her what the Bible said about what was happening to her, and to plead with her to stop what she was doing to hurt her testimony as a Christian. She insisted that there was a force behind her actions and that she felt out of control. She pleaded with me to pray over her. Reluctantly, I agreed. As I was praying, a demon began to manifest. I had never dealt with a demon in another person before, and did not know what to do. I was afraid, and I screamed at the demon, commanding it to leave. Then I noticed that her mouth was moving. I stopped praying, and heard her say, "Now that you want me to leave her, where do you want me to go?" Her natural voice was high-pitched as one would expect for a woman, but now she spoke with a voice as low as that of a man with a low voice. The demon left, and I was relieved.

Some believers take issues with my experience with this new convert, claiming that a Christian cannot have demonic oppressions in his or her life. What I am doing is relating her experience and not arguing theological issues. I do not fully understand these things, but I do know that Jesus had healed a woman who had a spirit of infirmity. He said to her, "Woman, you are loosed from your infirmity." She was healed, but the leader of the synagogue where Jesus healed her was upset because He had healed her on the Sabbath. Jesus defended his action by saying that she was a daughter of Abraham—a child of God—and deserved to be healed even on the Sabbath day (Luke 13:10-17). She was a child of God, a daughter of Abraham, but still she had a spirit of infirmity.

The voice of the demon that spoke to me through the new convert stayed in my head for a while, as I wondered about my own experience and what was going on in my life. Praying in tongues and studying the Scriptures took away most of my concerns about these things. Since then, God has given me many opportunities to cast out demons and to see men and women who want God in their lives freed from Satan's oppression. I have lost my fear of demons and their activities in the world.

Teaching other believers

Praying in the spirit gave me so much boldness and confidence with understanding that I started to question some of my beliefs that cannot be supported by the Word of God. I wondered out loud why ordinary Christians could not perform miracles like some seasoned ministers, although the Bible seems to indicate that every believer should be able to do what Jesus did. I became interested in the gifts of the Holy Spirit, and decided to teach about them in my Sunday school class. I was amazed at how God confirmed His Word. Some in the class, ordinary believers, prophesized for the first time, speaking words of knowledge and words of wisdom, just as I thought should be possible. I am currently still living some of the words of prophecy that were spoken over me in that class. The Scriptures became a living reality.

Home in Nigeria in 1988

I spent all of 1988 in Nigeria waiting to return to the United States to do a doctoral program at Texas A&M University. I

grew a lot as a Christian worker because I had much time to do ministry work, which I had always loved doing. I spent much time praying, teaching, and freeing people from demonic oppression and possession. It was during this time the Lord started talking to me about believing in Him enough to pray for those who are sick in the body. Divine healing was a matter that I did not fully understand, and I thought I would leave it to those the Lord was already using in that area of the Lord's work. I had become very comfortable praying with people to receive the Holy Spirit and freeing individuals from demonic activities. It became almost a daily affair, and I was fully enjoying the boldness I felt in Him. I woke up early each day to spend my hour of prayer with the Lord just to prepare myself for whatever God had in store for me that day. People came for help and received it because the Lord was working with me daily.

People were getting saved and filled with the Holy Spirit. I decided to start a Bible study group in my home since I had a lot of young people interested in what I was doing and in the power of God. That Bible study group later became a church when a friend of mine, Dr. Daniel Bernard of Somebody Cares, Tampa Bay, Florida, decided to live in Nigeria as a missionary.

Leave the casting out of demons to us

When I arrived in Nigeria late December, 1987, I discovered that my Christian brothers and sisters had been given a lot of knowledge about how to cast out demons and free those who were tormented. I had knowledge of how to deal with them, but not a lot of experience with it. My fellow Christians became aware that I could help those who wanted to receive the Holy Spirit, but they were not sure about my understanding with regards to casting out demons. They said, "Leave the casting out of demons to us; we will bring people to you for the baptism of the Holy Spirit after they have been freed from demons." But I was confident that I could cast out any demon in the name of Jesus because Jesus had said this was possible. Moreover, I had discovered that those who had a demon giving them trouble before they were saved got delivered quickly when I prayed with them to receive the Holy Spirit. The demons manifested when I encouraged the people to ask for the baptism of the Spirit with speaking in tongues. Then it was easy for me to cast the demons out. The individuals then received the Holy Spirit without any demonic manifestation afterwards.

Before long, it became known in our little town that I could cast out demons, and people came to me both to receive the baptism of the Holy Spirit and to be delivered from demons. It was a busy time in my life working with people in the kingdom of God. Every day, I prayed and studied the Word of God and waited for people to come with their problems. I had to depend on the Holy Spirit a lot when I was confronted with problems that I had not dealt with before. I discovered that I could never become an expert. Every problem was different. Many times I cried out to God in my heart for answers while dealing with an unfamiliar problem. Outwardly I exuded confidence, but inside I was crying out for wisdom and understanding. God never failed me.

Divine healing unveiled

I had always been very interested in divine healing as revealed in the gospels of Jesus' life, and in the life of the apostles as recorded in the book of Acts. In crusades in Africa, I had seen people testifying that God had healed them of some disease or other, but I did not know those individuals to be sick before they were healed in the meetings. My heart's desire for a very long time was to see someone healed. It did not matter who was doing the praying or who was healed, I just wanted to see a miracle.

After I began to pray frequently in tongues, my desire for the miraculous grew. I read books about divine healing by T.L. Osborn, E.W. Kenyon, and F.F. Bosworth, all great people who God used, and one of them still being used today to bring comfort to the sick by the power of the Christ. The more I read, the more interested I became in the power of Christ to heal the sick.

One night in 1998, I woke up with some understanding that I was able, by the power of the Lord Jesus Christ, to bring healing to the deaf and cause the dumb to speak. This was the same year that the Lord talked to me about leaving my secular job to go into full-time ministry, although He made it clear that it was not yet time.

The final call came in the year 2000. In June of that year, I left secular work to do full-time ministry. I immediately travelled to my native country, Nigeria, where I knew my pastor friends would allow me to minister to the people from their pulpits. The Lord had shown me much about healing over the years as I studied and prayed. I wanted to prove what God had been showing me in my Spirit. I had always wanted to see a real miracle, and now I wanted God to perform one through me. Almost immediately, during my very first service in Lagos, a young man who had injured his back in a severe car accident and suffered pain for four years was healed. Several others were healed in those meetings in Lagos. I had the same results in Benin City, Sapele, Agbor, and Warri.

In Warri, a lady who had broken her leg a week or so before the meeting came limping into the service. God healed her, and she testified with joy, running all over the church as she testified. It did not take long before the Nigerian ministers began to introduce me as a healing evangelist, while in my mind I asked, "Who, me?" God had fulfilled His Word to me. God is faithful to His Word.

God is the one who does the healing, but just knowing that, as a believer, will not make the healing work. A heart understanding of the message as we study the Word of God with prayer is what builds faith to cause miracles to take place in our ministry and our lives as witnesses of the resurrection and power of our Lord Jesus Christ.

Why does God not perform the same miracles in America?

I returned to the United States of America from Nigeria after my first trip to Nigeria as a full time minister of the gospel with videos of testimonies of those who had been saved, healed, delivered from demons, and filled with the Holy Spirit. After I had testified about what God did in Africa during my trip, someone asked me why God does not do the same kinds of miracles in America. I was not expecting a question like that. I did not know how to answer it. I knew that there have been divine healings in the ministry of many in America, but I took the challenge and went to God in prayer, asking Him to do with me what He had done in Nigeria.

God answered that prayer, and in churches, crusade meetings, and with individuals on a one to one basis in Texas, Florida, Georgia, New York, South Carolina, and everywhere I had the opportunity to preach, people were healed. Jesus is the same yesterday, today, and forever. I believe that none of these experiences would have been a part of my life if I had not made the decision to pray in tongues every time I pray, and to do so for as long as my schedule for that day allows.

LANGUAGE FROM HEAVEN

Sir, you may stop praying, I can hear you

I was invited to preach in a church in Cordele, Georgia, after my first trip to Nigeria. I spent a lot of time praying with the pastor the evening before the next day's service. Many people were healed in that meeting including a woman with a heart condition who was healed while I was speaking. God healed her before I had the privilege to pray for her. This is the nature of the God we serve. He loves to bless His people. He loves to heal those who are sick and oppressed.

After I had prayed with a few people, a lady came up with her daughter, crying. She informed me that her daughter was completely deaf in one ear, and almost completely deaf in the other. I felt compassion in my heart when I looked on her and her daughter. I now know that that was the compassion of Christ at work in me. I told her to stop crying because her daughter would be healed. I started to pray for her. Sometimes I yell when I pray, and this was one of those occasions. I was yelling as I prayed, but then I noticed that the young girl was saying something to me. I listened, and the whole church heard her say to me, "Sir, you may stop praying now, I can hear you." Everyone laughed, but I was glad that Jesus had healed her, and that He is willing to use anyone who wants to be used. The power of the Holy Spirit gave me the boldness not to be afraid of the names of sicknesses and diseases people have, but to have confidence in the power of the name of Jesus. Praying in tongues regularly will build this confidence in every believer. "But you, beloved, building yourselves up on your most holy faith, praying in the Holy Spirit" (Jude 1:20).

The power of the tongues to deliver

I stumbled onto a powerful secret when I began to pray with people to receive the Holy Spirit. I noticed that sometimes, at the point when I encourage them to believe and to step out in faith, praying in tongues, a demon manifests. Whenever this happens, it was easy to cast out the demon, and then go through the process of helping the believer receive the Holy Spirit a second time. After the demon is cast out, I usually will not see any other manifestation as the person begins to speak in tongues. This happened in Nigeria in 1988 with a young woman whom I was told was possessed with a powerful demon. She wanted to be free, but the ministers in Nigeria trusted me only with regards to helping people receive the baptism of the Holy Spirit. My minister friend told me that she had received Christ as her Lord and Savior, but that she needed to be freed from the demons in her life before praying to be baptized with the Holy Spirit. I was told that once they had freed her of the demons in her life, they would bring her to me to receive the Holy Spirit. I agreed.

Weeks passed, and I heard nothing more about this young woman. Then one day the minister showed up with her at my home. He said she had been freed from all the demons that troubled her, and she was now ready to be filled with the Holy Spirit. I shared with the young woman about the Holy Spirit, and what she must do to receive. She understood the message well, so we proceeded to pray for her, but when I told her to step out in faith to speak in tongues, a demon manifested powerfully. Together, my minister friend and I went after the demon in the name of Jesus, and he left her immediately. We went through the process again briefly, and then she began to pray in tongues beautifully without any demonic manifestation. She was free! A few weeks later, I saw the same woman at a church service worshipping God with such joy and excitement that I could not help but give God glory for the power of the Holy Spirit at work in her life.

In a small village called Adeje near Warri, Delta State, Nigeria I held a meeting in a small church. Among those in attendance was a woman who had a condition that had made her sick for twenty-five years. She was probably about sixty-five years old. I knew nothing about her condition. I spoke about the Holy Spirit and prayed for the people to receive the Holy Spirit. She had a somewhat violent reaction as she started to pray in tongues, but that ceased after a while. She said nothing to anyone during the few days of the meetings, but on the last day, she brought an offering to thank God for her healing. She was delivered from the demon that had kept her bound in sickness for twenty-five years when she received the baptism of the Holy Spirit.

CHAPTER 15

THE HOLY SPIRIT

Who is the Holy Spirit?

The Holy Spirit is God. He is the third person in the Godhead. He is not lesser than the Father or the Son in any way. The Bible tells us that God is Spirit, and that Spirit is the Holy Spirit (John 4:24). He is equal in all respects to the Father and the Son. He was there at the beginning of the creation of the world.

> In the beginning God created the heavens and the earth. The earth was without form, and void; and darkness was on the face of the deep. And the Spirit of God was hovering over the face of the waters.
>
> —Genesis1:1-2

Before the Father spoke the Word, the Spirit was already at work, hovering over the surface of the waters, waiting for the Father's command. The Holy Spirit is the One who takes the Father's spoken Word and manifests it in the physical realm. His work and position are extremely important for life in the natural world. He takes from the unseen world and brings it into the seen, where man can see, taste, hear, feel, or smell—where man can enjoy. The more humans cooperate with the Holy Spirit in light of the Word of God, the more of the supernatural will be observed in the natural world. The Father spoke the Word, and the Holy Spirit gave substance to the spoken word in the natural world. This is just what happens to those who have been filled with the Holy Spirit. We do the speaking, and the Holy Spirit gives the utterance (Acts 2:4).

Divided tongues of fire

When the Holy Spirit was first introduced to us in the Scriptures, He was hovering over the face of the waters (Genesis 1:2). He had no physical form. However, in the baptism of the Lord Jesus, men were able to use their God-given senses to hear the Father speak, see the Son in human form, and see the Holy Spirit descending from heaven and alighting on the Son in the form of a dove. This was the first time in the Scriptures that the Holy Spirit is given a physical form. Before this, He was the breath of God, like the wind.

On the day of Pentecost, the Holy Spirit came to the earth in all of His fullness. There was a sound from heaven like that of a mighty rushing wind, and it filled the house where the one hundred and twenty disciples of Jesus had gathered to wait for His coming. There He appeared to them as divided tongues of fire—one sat on each of the disciples. The result was that all one hundred and twenty disciples were filled with the Holy Spirit, and began to speak in tongues as the Holy Spirit gave utterance. This was the last emblem of the Holy Spirit as seen on the earth. I believe that it is significant that when the Holy Spirit filled or anointed those who believed in the Savior at the first, they saw Him in the realm of the senses as tongues. In my mind, God was indicating that tongues and the baptism of the Holy Spirit cannot be separated. When you are filled with the Holy Spirit, tongues must be a part of your experience. The tongue is the most powerful organ of our body. The Bible tells us that it holds the power of death and life in it (Proverbs 18:21). God wants to use this powerful part of our body to speak supernatural words to transform our realm of the natural into the realm of the supernatural in order that His will might be done in our lives and in the world.

Baptized with the Holy Spirit and fire

> I indeed baptize you with water unto repentance, but He Who is coming after me is mightier than I, whose sandals I am not worthy to carry. He will baptize you with the Holy Spirit and fire.
>
> —Matthew 3:11

John's baptism was only with water, but Jesus' will be with the Holy Ghost and with fire. On the day of Pentecost, the Holy Spirit descended from heaven with the sound of a mighty rushing wind. I think that He could not wait to get to the earth to begin His work in man. He appeared to the disciples as divided tongues of fire. This, I believe is the baptism of fire. He sets our tongues on fire to speak in tongues to God in prayer (1 Corinthians 14:2), and to speak to men in our natural tongues to give them the knowledge of the Savior, accompanied by signs and wonders for salvation. With the coming of the Holy Spirit, God is giving us a tongue of fire, and the fire is the fire of life, not of death. When we speak in tongues, we breathe life into our natural bodies to empower them to do the will of God on the earth.

> For I will give you a mouth and wisdom which all your adversaries will not be able to contradict or resist.
>
> —Luke 21:15

> I will put My Spirit within you and cause you to walk in My statutes, and you will keep My judgments and do them.
>
> —Ezekiel 36:27

The baptism of the Holy Ghost and fire is what gives the believer advantage over the forces of the Evil One. Jesus said that we will receive power when the Holy Spirit has come upon us, and we will then be transformed into His witnesses, with power to bring people to the knowledge of the saving grace of the Lord Jesus Christ. Our faith in this power will be unstoppable.

> Behold, I give you the authority to trample on serpents and scorpions, and over all the power of the enemy, and nothing shall by any means hurt you.
>
> —Luke 10:19

The breath of God

God formed man out of the dust and breathed into his nostrils the breath of life, and man became a living being (Genesis 2:7). The breath of God brought man to life. The Spirit of God is the breath of God, and the Spirit is God. The dust that was formed by God was touched by the essence of God when His breath touched it, and everything the Spirit touches comes alive.

> The Spirit of God has made me, and the breath of the Almighty gives me life.
>
> —Job 33:4

> It is the Spirit who gives life; the flesh profits nothing. The words that I speak to you are spirit, and they are life.
>
> —John 6:63

In chapter 37 of Ezekiel, the Spirit of the Lord carried the prophet into a valley filled with dry bones. The Lord asked the prophet to prophesy to the dry bones. He did, and the dry bones came together, bone to bone. Muscles came onto those bones, and flesh grew, and skin covered the bones. But that was all that happened; the beings formed by his prophecy had no life in them. They were like Adam after God formed him from the dust of the earth (Genesis 2:7).

The Lord then commanded the prophet to prophesy to the breath, asking it to come from the four winds, and breathe on the slain people. The prophet prophesied, and life came into them, and they stood up on their feet, an exceedingly great army (Ezekiel 37:1-10).

The breath spoken of here is the breath of the Holy Spirit, the same breath that touched Adam after he was formed from the dust of the earth and made him a living being. I believe that a Christian is made a new creature when he receives Christ as Lord and Savior, but he becomes a potentially powerful witness for Christ when he allows himself to be filled with the Holy Spirit in baptism (Acts 1:8).

From the unseen to the seen

Everything that is seen in the natural world came from the unseen world. It takes a word from God and the workings of the Holy Spirit to bring what is already present in the Spirit realm into our natural world where it can be seen, felt, tasted, smelled, and heard. The story of creation in Genesis demonstrates this. In the beginning, God created the heavens and the earth. The earth was without form, and void, and darkness was on the face of the deep. The Holy Spirit hovered over the surface of the waters (Genesis 1:1-2). God gave the Word, and the Holy Spirit did His work. There was darkness on the surface of the deep. The darkness first had to be eliminated before anything else could be done, so God's first words were, "Let there be light," and there was light, and the darkness that was on the surface of the deep disappeared (Genesis 1:30). I have already made it clear that the light in the beginning did not come from the Sun. The Sun was created on the fourth day. Deep calls out to deep (Psalm 42:7). Light cannot call out to darkness for anything that is good to happen; the darkness had to be eliminated before the creation of order.

The life of a sinner is without form, and void, and darkness exists on the face of his heart. The Word of God has been sent to bring the gospel of light to remove the darkness in his heart so that God can begin to build order into his life. The Holy Spirit is already on the earth hovering over the face of the deep in every human heart so that it can be enlightened with the word of God.

> And when He has come, He will convict the world of
> sin, and of righteousness, and of judgment.
>
> —John 16:8

The Bible tells us that in the beginning, before the creation of the seen world, was the Word. The Word was with God, and the Word was God (John 1:1). Jesus existed as the Word of God before the creation of the seen or natural world. For Him to be manifested and seen in the natural world, the angel Gabriel was sent to give the word of God to Mary. However, the word from God alone was not enough for Jesus' manifestation in the flesh. The Holy Spirit is the one that can take things from the unseen world and make them visible in the seen world where we live.

> And the angel answered and said to her, "The Holy Spirit will come upon you, and the power of the Highest will overshadow you; therefore, also, that Holy One who is to be born will be called the Son of God."
>
> —Luke 1:35

Paul told us that God has blessed us with every spiritual blessing in the heavenly places in Christ (Ephesians 1:3). The problem with all the spiritual blessings is that they are in heavenly places. However, although we are seated with Christ in the heavenly places according to the Scriptures, our dwelling place right now is on the earth (Ephesians 2:6). We need the blessings to meet us here on the earth where we live. We get these blessings into our lives by allowing the Holy Spirit to work with us, using these promises to make the blessings manifest in the natural world for us to enjoy.

The Spirit of wisdom

The Bible says wisdom is the principal thing, therefore get wisdom, and in all your getting get understanding (Proverb 4:7). Wisdom

is the master key to unlocking the secrets of successful living. The wisdom we are talking about here is not common sense. The Bible is talking about divine wisdom, spiritual wisdom. This wisdom cannot be found on earth. It comes from heaven, from the Lord. Solomon received this uncommon wisdom from God when the Lord visited him in a dream (1 Kings 3:5-13). He became the wisest man, apart from our Lord Jesus Christ, who ever lived. Solomon was not born with this wisdom. It was given to him. This was not natural wisdom, but supernatural wisdom. This is the wisdom necessary for success in every area of life. It is spiritual wisdom from the Holy Spirit.

> The Spirit of the Lord shall rest upon Him, the Spirit of wisdom and understanding, the Spirit of counsel and might, the Spirit of knowledge and of the fear of the Lord.
>
> —Isaiah 11:2

The Spirit of the Lord is the Spirit of wisdom and understanding. The prophecy in the above passage is about our Lord Jesus. This prophecy was fulfilled in His life and ministry. The Spirit of the Lord is the Spirit of counsel and might, all of which was evident in the ministry and life of our Lord Jesus. His answers to difficult questions posed to trap Him bring us face to face with uncommon wisdom, divine wisdom. According to the above passage it was a result of the Holy Spirit on Him.

Wisdom that comes from the Holy Spirit unlocks doors for miracles to take place. Those who grew up in Nazareth recognized and acknowledged that Jesus had received wisdom not common to man. They were amazed at His understanding and the signs that followed His ministry.

> And when the Sabbath had come, He began to teach in the synagogue. And many hearing Him were astonished, saying, "Where did this Man get these things? And what wisdom is this which is given to Him, that such mighty works are performed by His hands!
>
> —Mark 6:2

The mighty works were a result of the wisdom that was given to Him because of the presence of the Holy Spirit in His life. The people of Nazareth wanted to know where He got His wisdom; they wanted to know the nature of the wisdom that resulted in such mighty works being done by His hands. They were offended by Him because they were ignorant of the fact that it was as a result of the Spirit of the Lord on His life. Wisdom is indeed the principal thing.

When the seven were selected in Acts chapter 6 to serve tables, the apostles wanted men of good reputation, full of the Holy Spirit and wisdom. If they were full of the Holy Spirit, they would be full of wisdom. Stephen was one of the men chosen to serve tables; but when you are full of the Holy Spirit and wisdom, you will not be serving tables for a long time. Stephen, full of faith and power, did great wonders among the people (Acts 6:8). Stephen had the same Spirit that was on Jesus, so he had the wisdom to do the things Jesus did. Stephen had problems with some people who disagreed with what he had to say, but his wisdom was too much for them!

> Then there arose some from what is called the Synagogue of the Freedmen (Cyrenians, Alexandrians, and those from Cilicia and Asia), disputing with Stephen. And they were not able to resist the wisdom and the Spirit by which he spoke.
>
> —Acts 6:9-10

LANGUAGE FROM HEAVEN

The presence of the Holy Spirit is the reason for the wisdom present in the life of Jesus. Jesus had made a promise to all believers to give them uncommon wisdom.

> For I will give you a mouth and wisdom which all your adversaries will not be able to contradict or resist.
>
> —Luke 21:15

Joseph also was filled with the Spirit of wisdom from the Lord. Pharaoh spoke to his servant about Joseph, saying, "Can we find such a one as this, a man in whom is the Spirit of God?" To Joseph he said, "Inasmuch as God has shown you all this, there is no one as discerning and wise as you. You shall be over my house, and all my people shall be ruled according to your word; only in regard to the throne will I be greater than you" (Genesis 41:38-40). The Spirit of wisdom in your life will bring you promotion.

The power of the anointing

The Holy Spirit is the Spirit of Power. Jesus said you shall receive power when the Holy Spirit has come on you (Acts 1:8). This is the power the believer needs to do damage to the kingdom of darkness, in his life and in the lives of those he touches with the gospel of Jesus Christ. This is supernatural power, not muscle power.

I am sure many think that Samson's power came from his physical build. However, I believe Samson looked like every other man around him. This is why when he did things that natural men cannot do with natural strength, the people wanted to know the secret of his strength (Judges 16:4-5). His power was only evident when the Holy Spirit came upon him (Judges 14:5-6). His strength was supernatural. And we need supernatural strength to be able to enforce the defeat Jesus handed the Devil when He died on the cross and rose again from the grave on the third day. The Devil was defeated, but we need the power of the Holy Spirit to keep him in his place. We need to be filled with God's Holy Spirit.

The power of the anointing comes with the Holy Spirit's baptism. This is the power that enabled the disciples of Jesus Christ to fully preach the gospel of Jesus Christ with signs and wonders. Paul said, "For I will not dare to speak of any of those things which Christ has not accomplished through me, in word and deed, to make the Gentiles obedient—in mighty signs and wonders, by the power of the Spirit of God, so that from Jerusalem and round about to Illyricum I have fully preached the gospel of Christ" (Romans 15:18-19). The mighty wonders Paul performed were through the power of the Holy Spirit, and Paul spoke in tongues more than any other, at least at the church of Corinth.

When the Holy Spirit came upon Jesus after His baptism by John, He was filled with the Holy Spirit, and led into the wilderness to fast and be tempted by the Devil (Luke 4:1). After that period of fasting, Jesus returned from the wilderness with the power of the Holy Spirit (Luke 4:14). Also, when the Holy Spirit came upon Jesus, He was anointed by God, and the Father spoke, declaring Jesus to be His only begotten Son (Luke 3:22).

> How God anointed Jesus of Nazareth with the Holy Spirit and with power, who went about doing good and healing all who were oppressed by the devil, for God was with Him.
>
> —Acts 10:38

LANGUAGE FROM HEAVEN

The anointing of the Holy Spirit comes with the power to do good and to heal all who are oppressed by the Devil. It is clear then that when a man is anointed, he is to do two things; do good, and bring healing to those oppressed by the Devil. The anointing is a spiritual requirement for men to be able to handle the Devil effectively. Jesus did, and Peter, Paul, and the other disciples were also able to do so.

The seal of the believer

God has a seal on all who are His in the world. The Holy Spirit is the seal of God in the believer's life. This is what identifies a man as belonging to God. Satan and his angels can see the seal of God on a man or woman, and they know to respect the anointing.

> In Him you also trusted, after you heard the word of truth, the gospel of your salvation; in whom also, having believed, you were sealed with the Holy Spirit of promise.
> —Ephesians 1:13

> And do not grieve the Holy Spirit of God, by whom you were sealed for the day of redemption.
> —Ephesians 4:30

The believer is exhorted to be careful not to grieve the seal of God in his or her life. Why? The believer's life depends on the seal. The Holy Spirit is the One who is able to make the believer a wonder in the world. This is why God sent the Holy Spirit into the world: to make the believer a light on the earth. We must rely on His guidance to be effective witnesses of the resurrection our Lord Jesus Christ, and His power to save all who believe in His name.

Part of the blessing of Abraham that becomes an inheritance for all Gentile believers is the promise of the Spirit. The presence of the Holy Spirit in baptism for the Gentile believer is a clear sign that he has been redeemed from the curse of the Lord, and is now a part of the blessing of Abraham that God promised: "I will bless those who bless you, and I will curse him who curses you; and in you all the families of the earth shall be blessed" (Genesis 12:3).

> Christ has redeemed us from the curse of the law, having become a curse for us (for it is written, "Cursed is everyone who hangs on a tree"), that the blessing of Abraham might come upon the Gentiles in Christ Jesus, that we might receive the promise of the Spirit through faith.
>
> —Galatians 3:13-14

The anointing in you

Once you have been filled with the Holy Spirit, you become anointed. The anointing that the believer receives remains on him forever according to the promise of Jesus (John 14:16). It is the anointing that teaches us all things. John tells us:

> But the anointing which you have received from Him abides in you, and you do not need that anyone teach you; but as the same anointing teaches you concerning all things, and is true, and is not a lie, and just as it has taught you, you will abide in Him.
>
> —1 John 2:27

The Holy Spirit knows all things because He is God, and He dwells in us, anointing us for supernatural work. He searches the deep things of God and reveals them to us for our benefit. These deep things of God are freely given to us by Him (1 Corinthians 2:10-12). Everyone who has been filled with the Holy Spirit is anointed, and if the believer engages the Spirit in prayer and by study of the Word of God, the Spirit will teach him all things by opening the eyes of his understanding to know the hope of His calling, the riches of the glory of God's inheritance in the saints, and the exceeding greatness of His power toward us who believe, according to the working of His mighty power which He worked in Christ when He raised Him from the dead and seated Him at His right hand in the heavenly places, far above all principality and power and might and dominion, not only in this age but also in that which is to come (Ephesians 1:18-21).

The generator in you

Jesus said that we are the salt of the earth and the light of the world (Matthew 5:13-16). I believe he is saying that life on earth would be tasteless without Christians. The world would be in total darkness. We have the keys to the kingdom of God, a supernatural kingdom that has dominion and can change things in the kingdom of darkness for the good of those who believe.

> Arise, shine; for your light has come! And the glory of the Lord is Risen upon you. For behold, the darkness shall cover the earth, and deep Darkness the people; but the Lord will arise over you, and His glory will be seen upon you.
>
> —Isaiah 60:1-2

Dr. Goodluck Okotie-Eboh

168

This Scripture has been fulfilled. There is spiritual darkness covering the earth, but the Lord Jesus was raised from the dead to give the light of life to everyone who believes. He makes the believer the light of the world—not this little light of mine, but the light of the world. When Jesus gives, He gives the best, and He would never give anyone only a little light unless that was all he or she wanted. He has risen over the believer and His glory can be seen in every believer. It is up to the believer to rise and shine; our light has come!

In every spirit filled-believer is a powerful generator that can cause the light in him to shine for the world to see. The believer is built to be the light of the world. The believer needs power from the generator to cause the light to come on. The generator is the Holy Spirit in the believer by baptism. Praying is how the generator is turned on. Turn on the generator! Pray in tongues often, and spend much time doing it, as Paul did (1 Corinthians 14:18).

It is one thing to have a generator when it is dark all around you and there is no power, and it is another thing when the generator is tuned on. Light comes, and darkness disappears. The baptism of the Holy Spirit is a divine generator of power in the believer's life; to turn it on, the believer must pray in the Spirit. The gas is the Word of God. No wonder St. Jude said, "But you, beloved, building yourselves up on your most holy faith, praying in the Holy Spirit" (Jude 1:20). You cannot pray in the Holy Spirit without praying in tongues.

> For if I pray in a tongue, my spirit prays, but my understanding is unfruitful. What is the conclusion then? I will pray with the spirit, and I will also pray with the understanding. I will sing with the spirit, and I will also sing with the understanding.
>
> —1 Corinthians 14:14-15

LANGUAGE FROM HEAVEN

Paul had his generator turned on constantly. He said, "I thank my God I speak with tongues more than you all" (1 Corinthians 14:18). No wonder he was so powerful as a Christian witness in his understanding and his message. Many Christians have left their generators off for a very long time. They have no prayer life; they spend very little time in prayer, and when they do pray, they do so mostly with their understanding, and only for short periods of time. They do not know what it means to wait on the Lord. They are constantly going, chasing after things they cannot get. Maybe if they spent some time waiting on the Lord, the blessings they seek would chase after them and overtake them (Deuteronomy 28:2). I believe they would then stop running from pillar to post chasing things that could be delivered to them by God.

The distributor of the gifts of God

The Holy Spirit comes into each believer's life with potential gifts for the believer to tap into. These gifts are called the manifestations of the Holy Spirit. There are nine spiritual gifts as revealed to us in 1 Corinthians chapter 12. The Holy Spirit is the One who distributes these various gifts according to His will. These are supernatural gifts from the Helper as He helps us to reach the world for Christ: the gift of prophecy, the gift of tongues, the gift of interpretation of tongues, the word of wisdom, the word of knowledge, the discerning of spirits, faith, healing, and the working of miracles (1 Corinthians 12:8-10). The baptism of the Holy Spirit with speaking in tongues is the gateway into all of these gifts, which are available to every believer, according to the will of the Holy Spirit.

The wise and the foolish virgins

In chapter 25 of the book of Matthew, Jesus gave us the parable of the ten virgins. Five of the virgins were said to be foolish, and the other five wise. The only difference between the wise and the foolish virgins was the amount of oil they had with them as they waited for the bridegroom to take them to the celebration. Both sets of virgins had lamps. The lamps were supposed to be burning bright when the bridegroom returned. That was a requirement for them to be with him. The lamps needed oil to burn, but the foolish virgins did not have enough to take them through the waiting period, and so they could not go in to the celebration with the bridegroom when He arrived.

The oil represents the Holy Spirit in a believer's life. The lamp represents the believer's life and influence, and the virgin is the believer. Every wise believer must desire to have a greater anointing of the Holy Spirit in His life: more oil. The Bible says, "Do not quench the Spirit" (1 Thessalonians 5:19). It is foolishness not to seek more of the Holy Spirit in our lives as believers.

Building your life on the rock

Jesus said that He likened everyone who hears His teachings but fails to practice them to a foolish man who built his house on the sand. He likened the man who hears and puts His words into practice to a wise man who built his house on the rock. Both houses will be tested with natural disasters; rain, floods, and wind will beat on both houses. The house built on sand will fall, and great is the fall of it, but the house that is built on the rock will stand (Matthew 7:24-27).

Language from Heaven

Every individual, every family, every church, every city, every state, every country will be tested by the troubles of life. The ones who make it will be those who have built their foundation for living on the words of Jesus. The words of Jesus are the words of the Father, and they are carried out and fulfilled in the lives of every believer through the power of the Holy Spirit. The Holy Spirit is the power at work in us as Christians (Ephesians 3:20). I pray for all believers alive on the earth today to make room for the Helper to truly help him in every area of life. Amen! Pray often in tongues.